PIANO/VOCAL/GUITAR

P9-DBP-728

25 MODERN WORSHIP SONGS
FOR A NEW GENERATION

I COULD SING OF YOUR LOVE FOR-EVER™ 2

ISBN 0-634-07981-6

HAL•LEONARD® CORPORATION

7777 W. BLUEMOUND RD. P.O. BOX 13819 MILWAUKEE, WI 53213

Visit Hal Leonard Online at
www.halleonard.com

CONTENTS

AWAKEN THE DAWN

Words and Music by
STUART GARRARD

Moderately slow (⅜ feel)

Sing to the Lord ___ with all of your heart, ___
Sing to the Lord ___ with all of your mind, ___

___ sing of the glo — ry that's
___ with un — der — stand — ing give

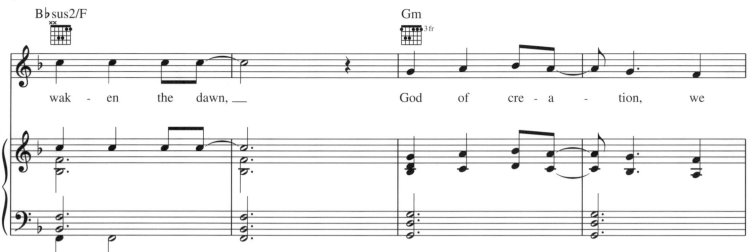

wak - en the dawn, ___ God of cre - a - tion, we

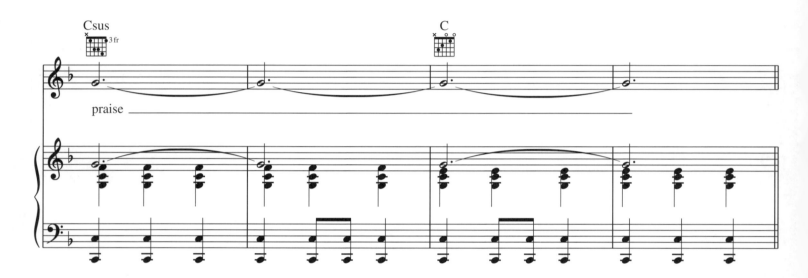

praise ___

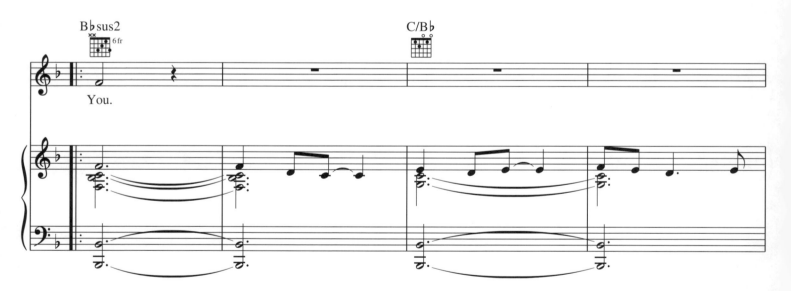

You.

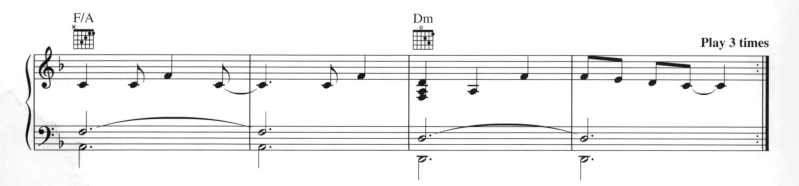

Play 3 times

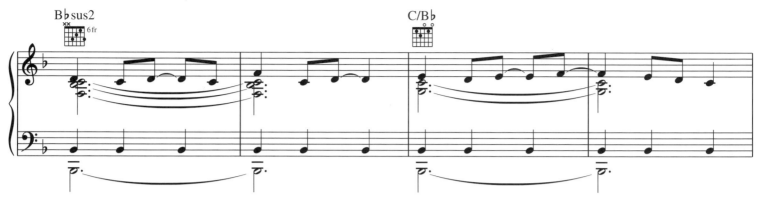

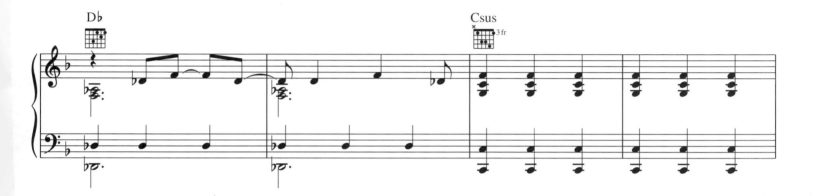

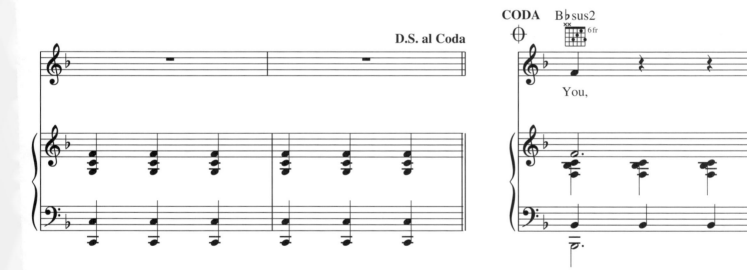

D.S. al Coda

CODA

You,

God of cre - a - tion, we praise You,

God of cre - a - tion, we praise _____

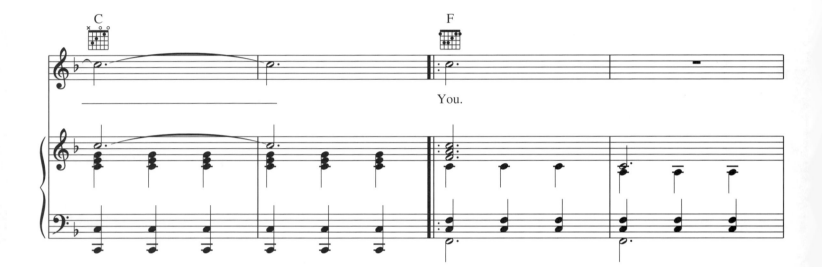

_____ You.

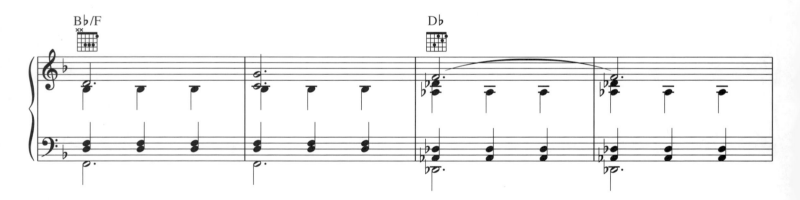

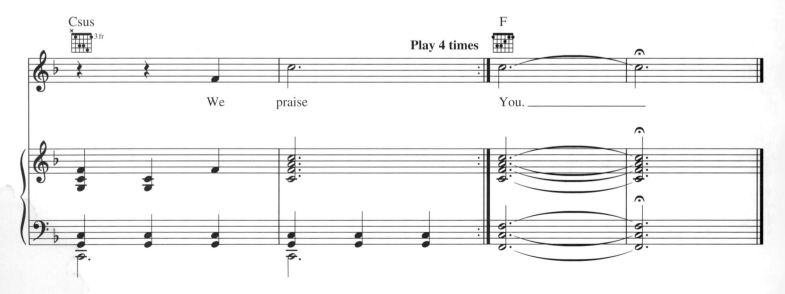

We praise You. _____

BREATHE

Words and Music by
MARIE BARNETT

- ly bread, _ Your ver - y Word _____

spo - ken _ to me. ____ ____ And

D.S. al Coda

CODA

I'm lost with-out _ You, _ I'm noth-ing with-

out You. _

BE GLORIFIED

Words and Music by LOUIE GIGLIO,
CHRIS TOMLIN and JESSE REEVES

COME, NOW IS THE TIME TO WORSHIP

Words and Music by
BRIAN DOERKSEN

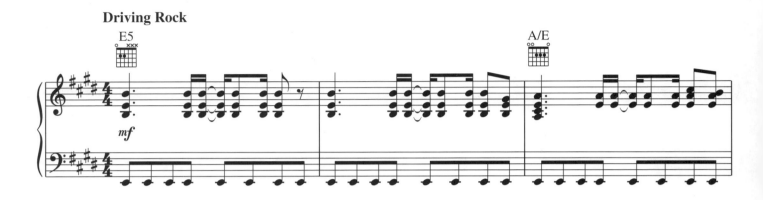

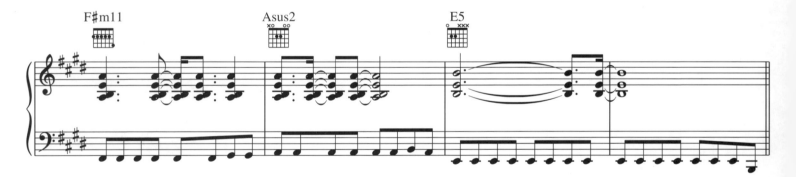

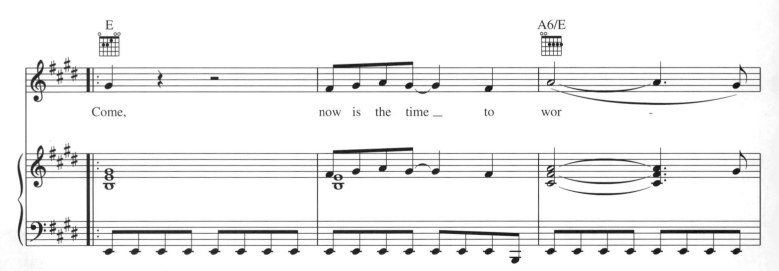

Come, now is the time ___ to wor -

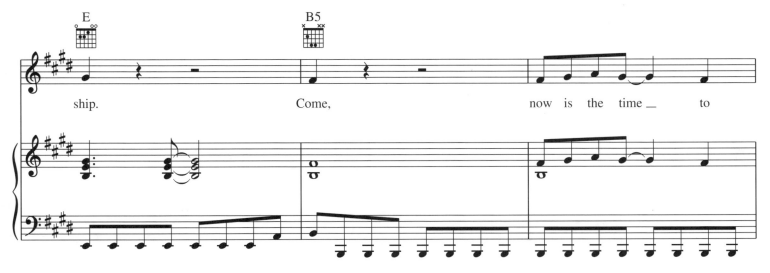

ship. Come, now is the time ___ to

give your _____ heart. Come,

just as you are, ___ to wor - ship.

Come, just as you are, ___ be - fore your _____

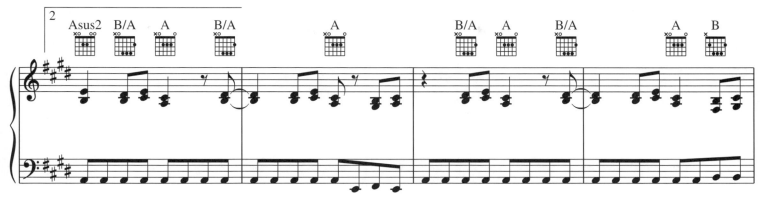

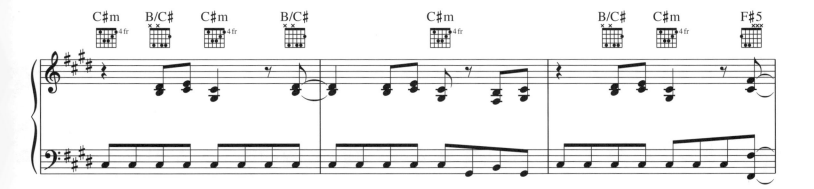

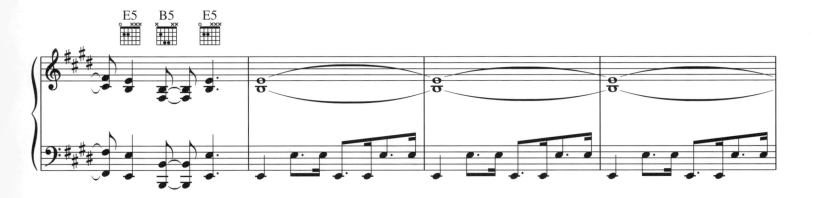

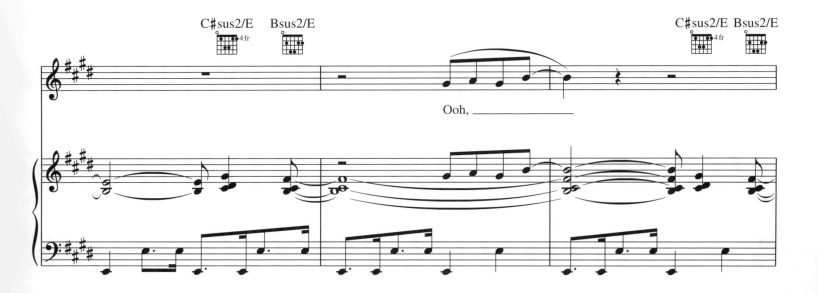

Ooh, _____

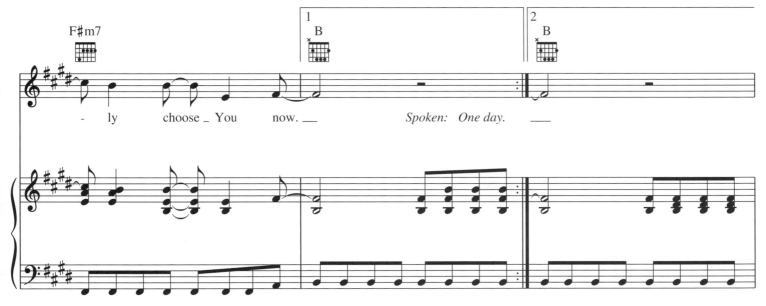

-ly choose _ You now. __   *Spoken: One day.* __

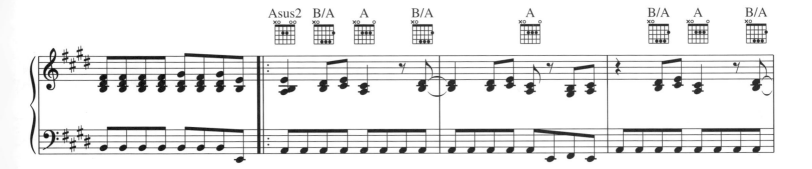

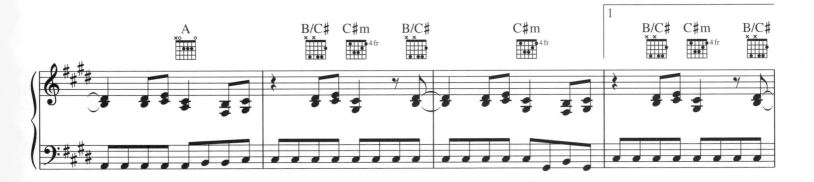

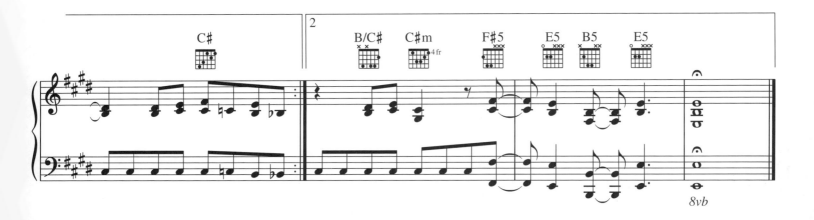

8vb

FOREVER

Words and Music by
CHRIS TOMLIN

Strong Rock beat

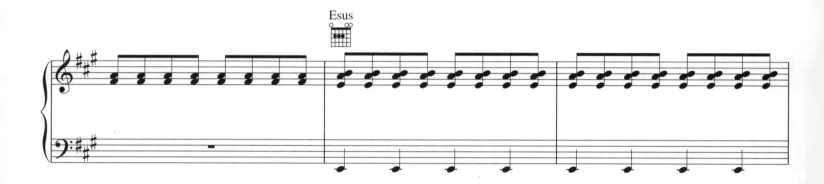

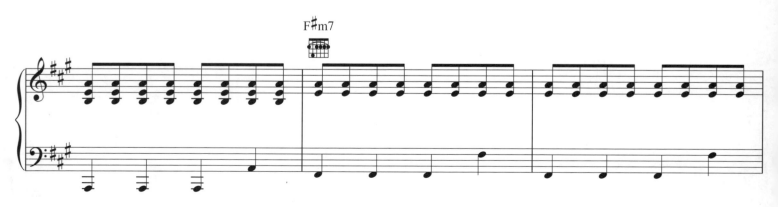

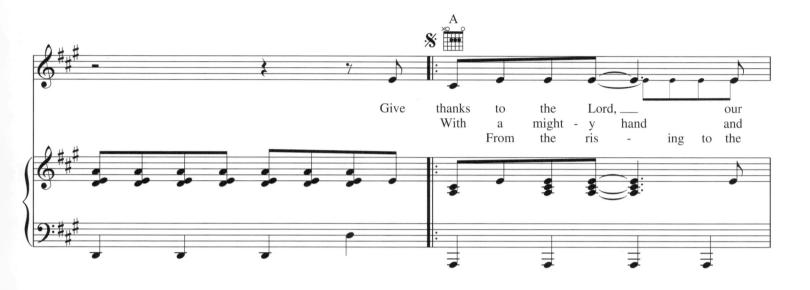

Give thanks to the Lord, ___ our
With a might - y hand and
From the ris - ing to the

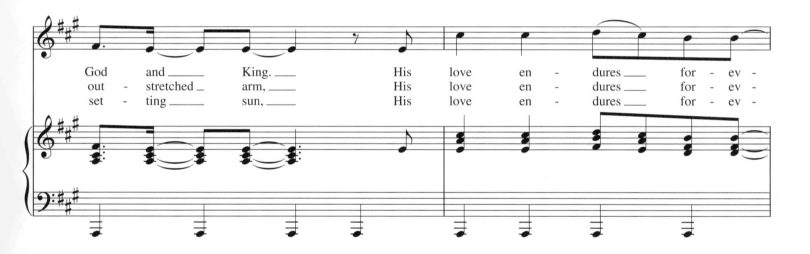

God and ___ King. ___ His love en - dures ___ for - ev -
out - stretched _ arm, ___ His love en - dures ___ for - ev -
set - ting ___ sun, ___ His love en - dures ___ for - ev -

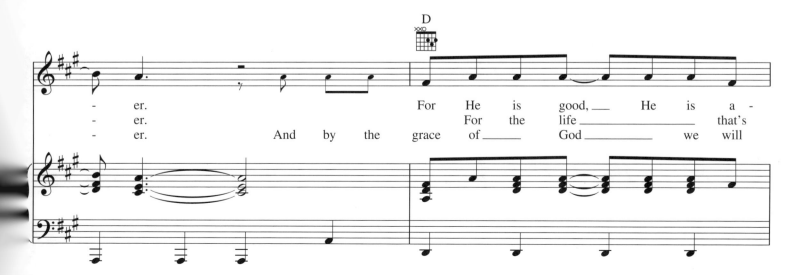

- er. For He is good, ___ He is a -
- er. For the life _____ that's
- er. And by the grace of _____ God _____ we will

bove all ___ things. ___ His love en - dures ___ for - ev - er.
been re - born, ___ His love en - dures ___ for - ev - er.
car - ry ___ on. ___ His love en - dures ___ for - ev - er.
Sing

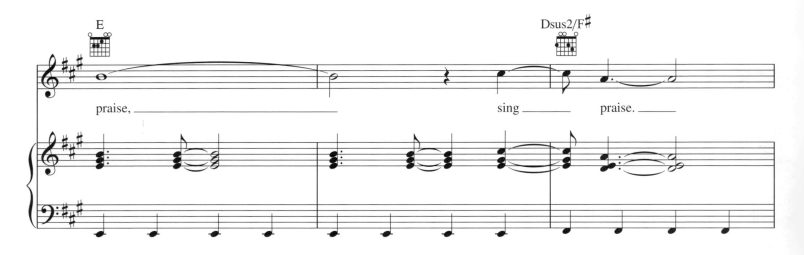

praise, _____ sing _____ praise. _____

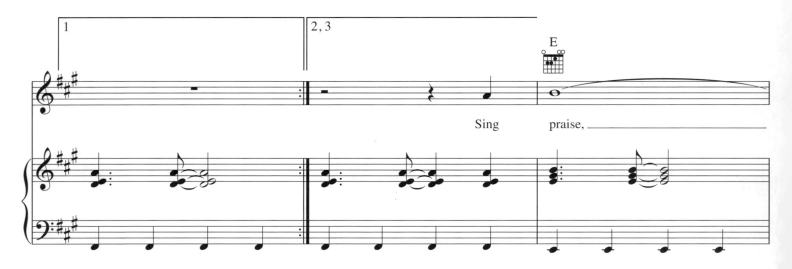

Sing praise, _____

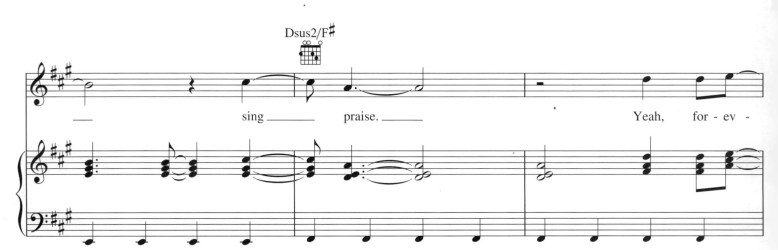

___ sing _____ praise. _____ Yeah, for - ev -

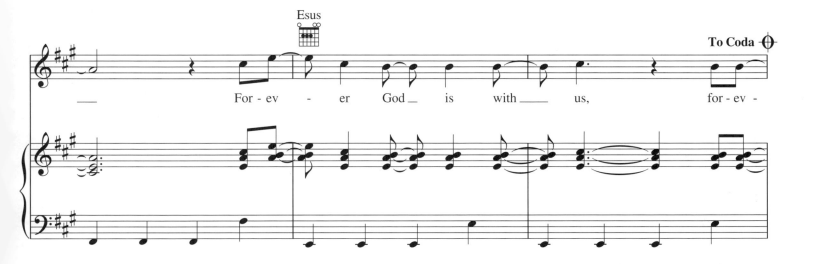

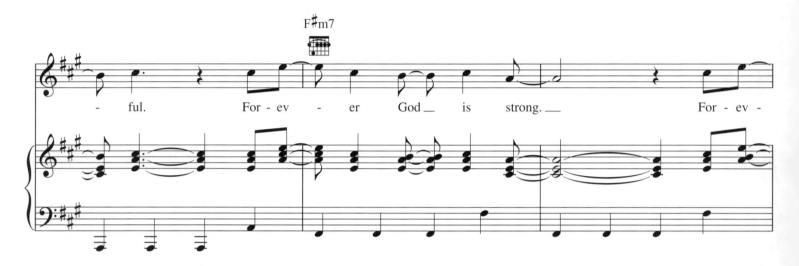

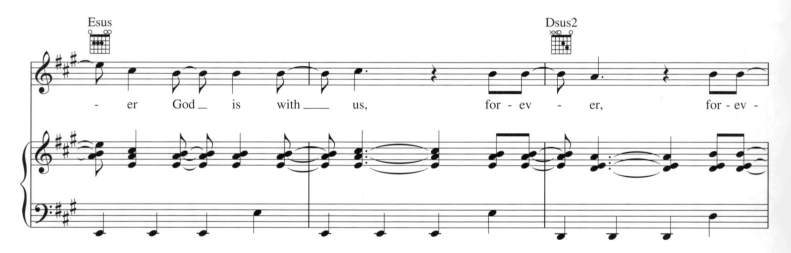

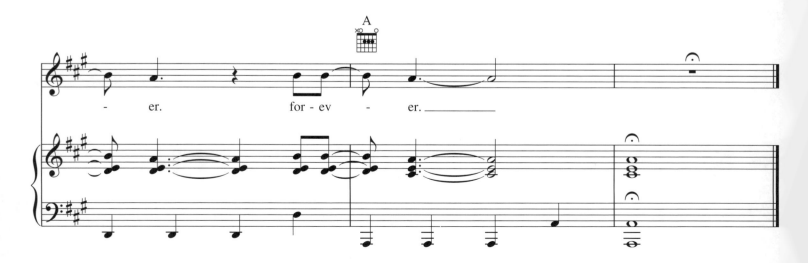

GIVE US CLEAN HANDS

Words and Music by
CHARLIE HALL

dols. So give us clean hands ___ and give us pure ___ hearts. ___

___ Let us not lift our souls ___ to an - oth -

- er. And give us clean hands ___ and give us pure ___ hearts. ___

___ Let us not lift our souls ___ to an - oth -

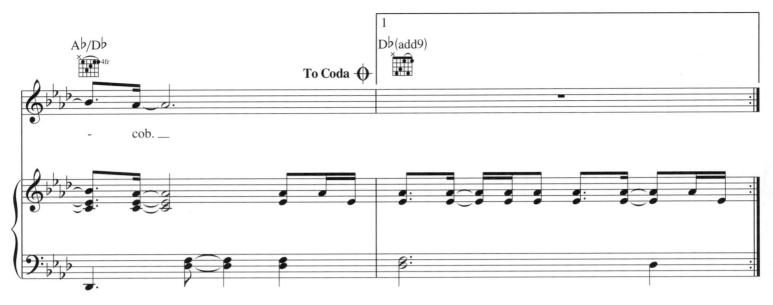

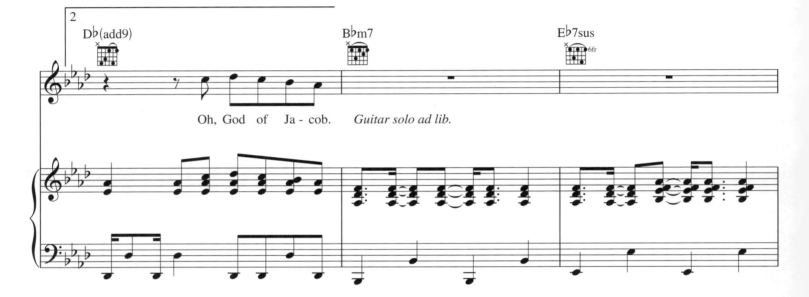

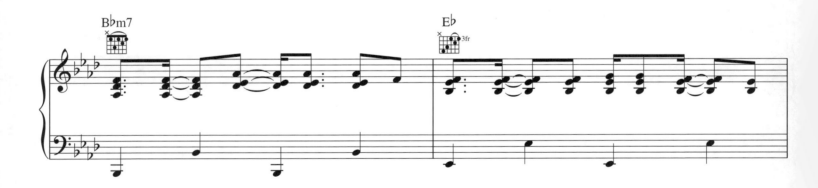

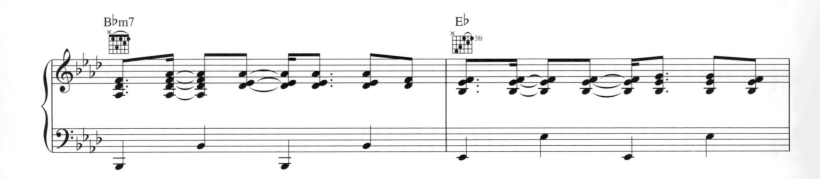

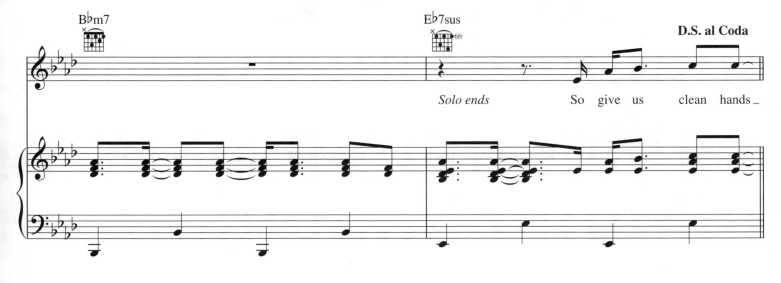

THE HEART OF WORSHIP

Words and Music by
MATT REDMAN

HERE I AM TO WORSHIP

Words and Music by
TIM HUGHES

Moderately slow

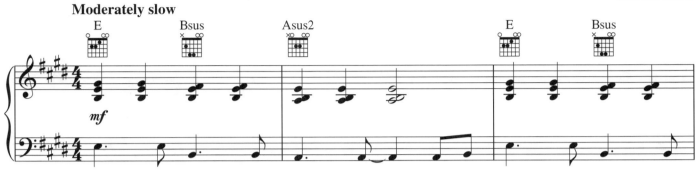

Light of the World, You stepped down in-to dark - ness,
King of all days, oh so high - ly ex - alt - ed,

o - pened my eyes, let me ___ see. ___ Beau - ty that made this ___
glo - rious in heav - en a - bove. ___ Hum - bly You came to the

heart a - dore ___ You, hope of a life spent with ___ You. ⌡
earth You cre - a - ted, all for love's sake be - came ___ poor. ⌡

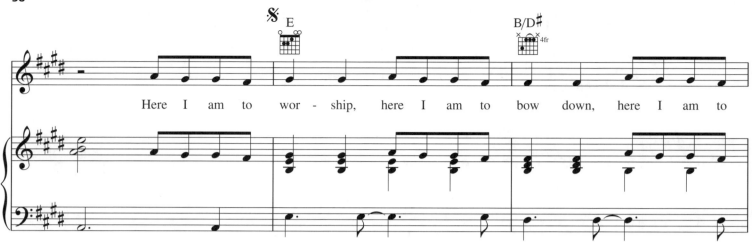

Here I am to wor-ship, here I am to bow down, here I am to

say that You're my God. ___ You're al-to-geth-er love-ly, al-to-geth-er

wor-thy, al-to-geth-er won-der-ful to me. ___

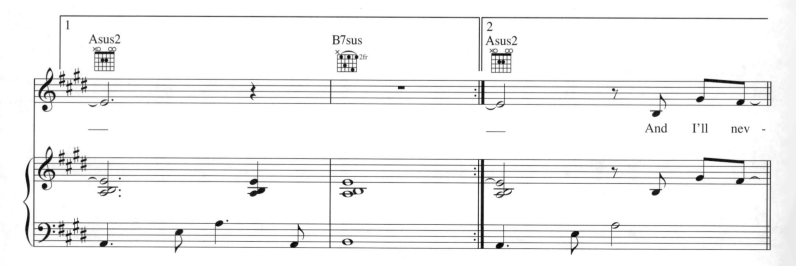

1
Asus2   B7sus   2
                                          Asus2

___   ___   And I'll nev-

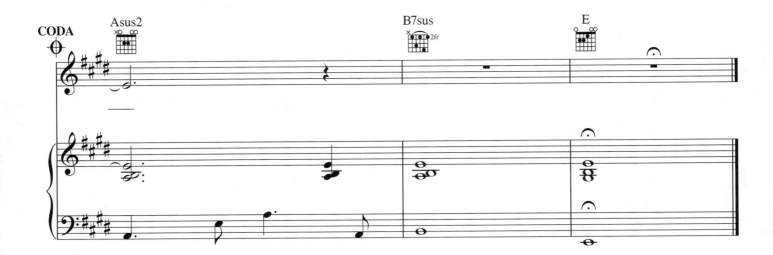

HOW DEEP THE FATHER'S LOVE FOR US

Words and Music by
STUART TOWNEND

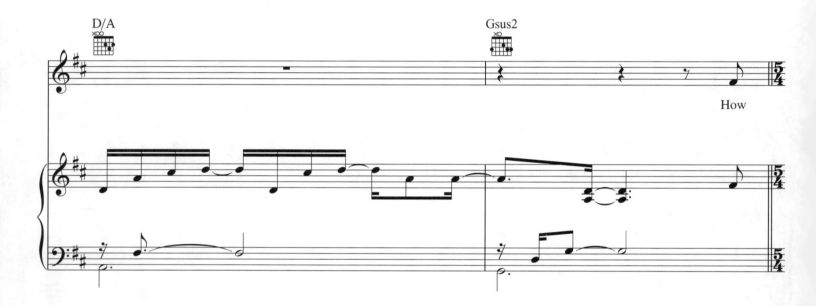

deep the Fa-ther's love for us; how vast be-yond all meas-ure that
hold the man up-on a cross, my sin up-on His shoul-ders. A-
will not boast in an-y-thing, no gifts, no pow'r, no wis-dom, but

He should give His on-ly Son to make a wretch His treas - ure. How
shamed, I hear my mock-ing voice call out a-mong the scoff - ers. It
I will boast in Je - sus Christ, His death and res - ur - rec - tion. What

great the pain of sear - ing loss. The Fa - ther turns His face a-way as
was my sin that held Him there un - til it was ac - com - plished. His
should I gain from His re - ward? I can - not give an an - swer, but

wounds which mar the Cho - sen One bring man - y sons to glo -
dy - ing breath has brought me life. I know that it is fin -
this I know with all my heart: His wounds have paid my ran -

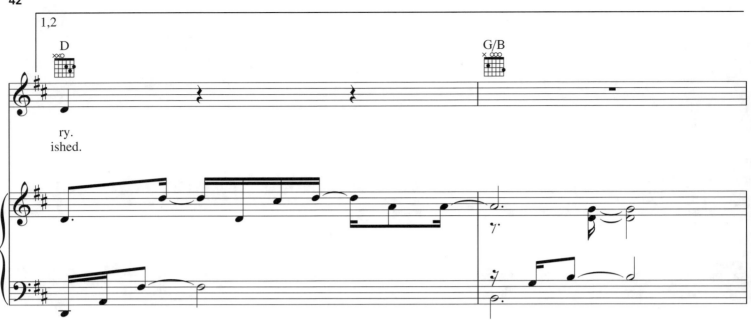

ry.
ished.

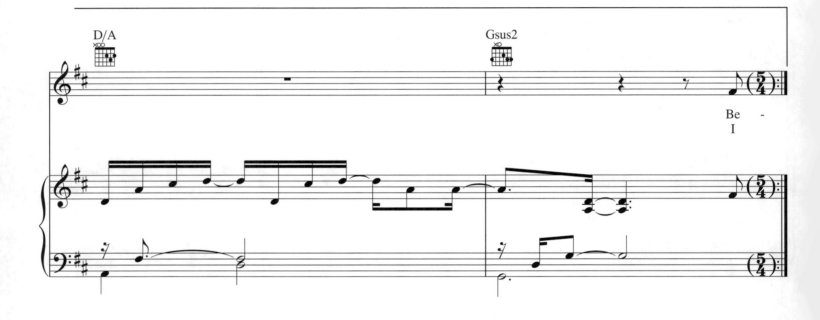

Be -
I

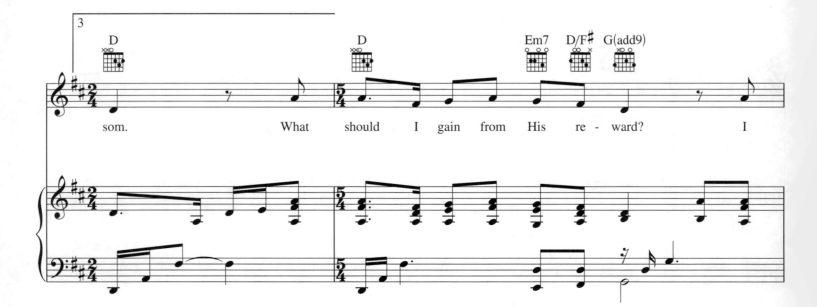

som.   What should I gain from His re - ward?   I

can - not give an an - swer, but this I know with all my heart: His

wounds have paid my ran - som.

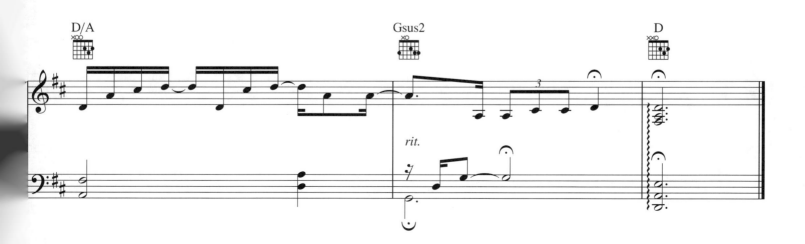

rit.

HUNGRY
(Falling on My Knees)

Words and Music by
KATHRYN SCOTT

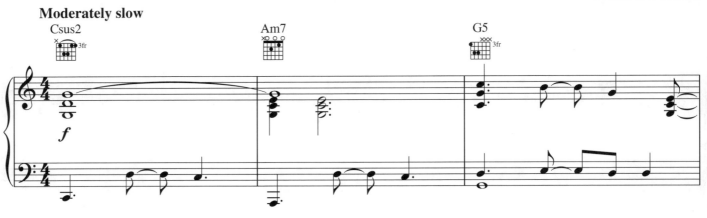

Moderately slow

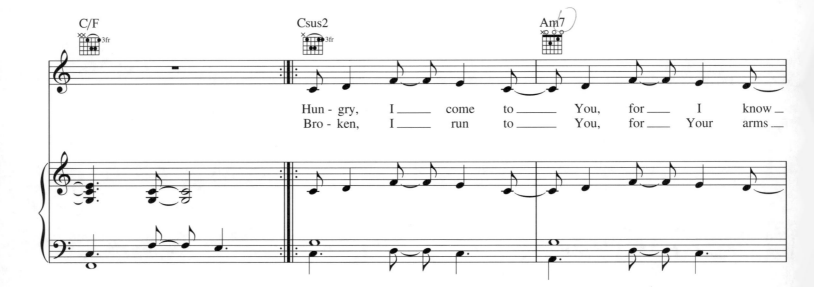

Hun - gry, I ___ come to ___ You, for ___ I know ___
Bro - ken, I ___ run to ___ You, for ___ Your arms

___ You sat - is - fy. ___ I am emp - ty but ___
___ are o - pen wide. ___ I am wea - ry but ___

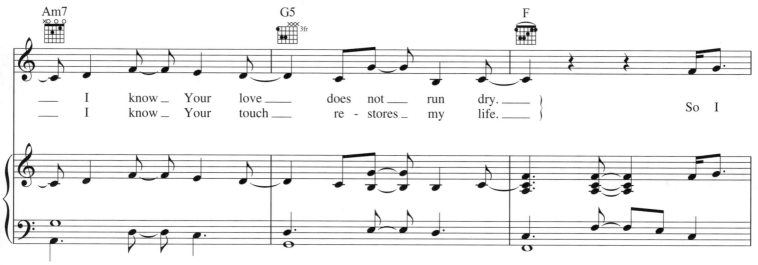

I know Your love does not run dry.
I know Your touch re-stores my life.
So I

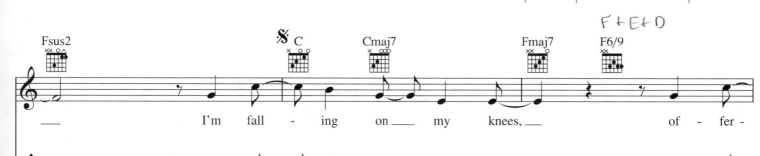

wait for You. So I wait for You.

I'm fall - ing on my knees, of - fer -

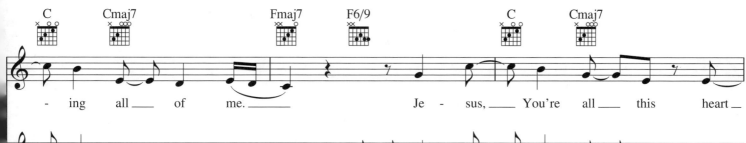

- ing all of me. Je - sus, You're all this heart

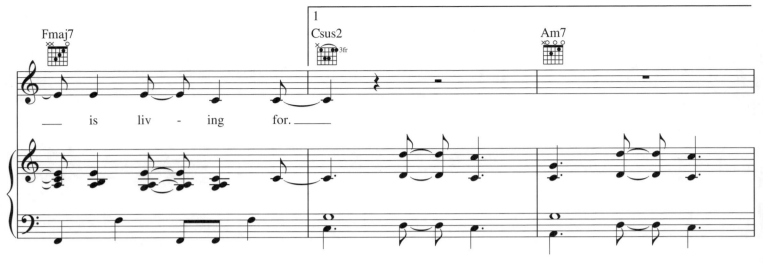

is liv - ing for.

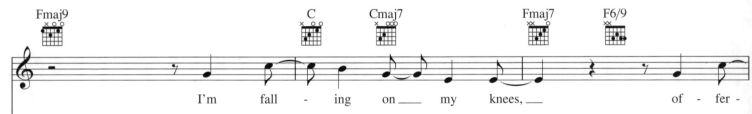

I'm fall - ing on my knees, of - fer -

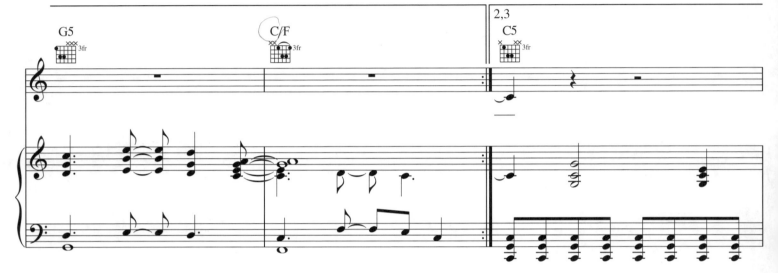

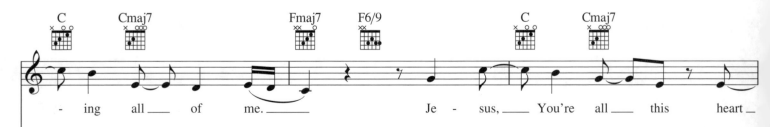

- ing all of me. Je - sus, You're all this heart

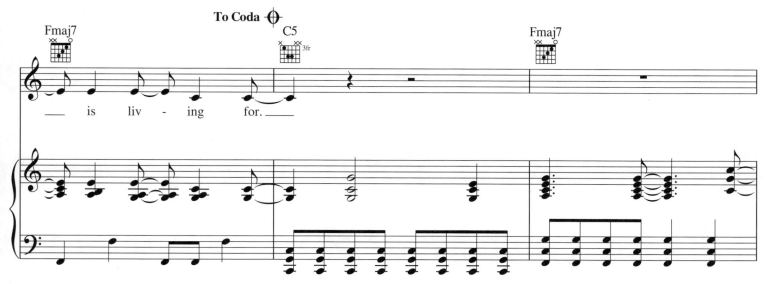

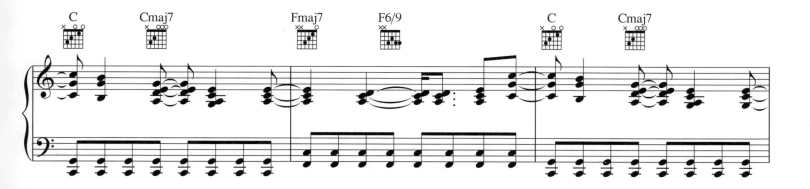

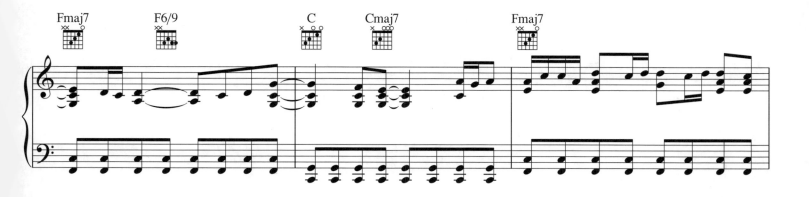

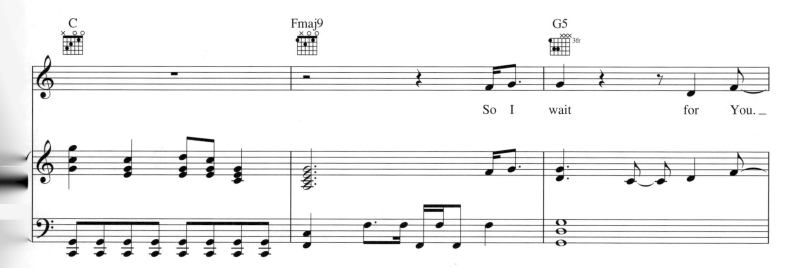

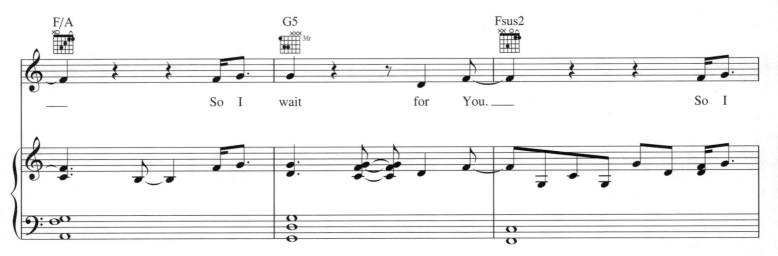

So I wait for You. ____ So I

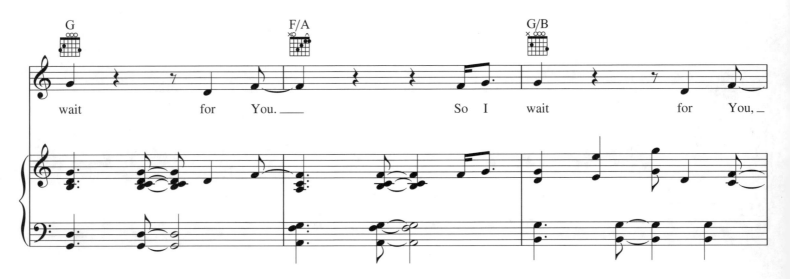

wait for You. ____ So I wait for You, ___

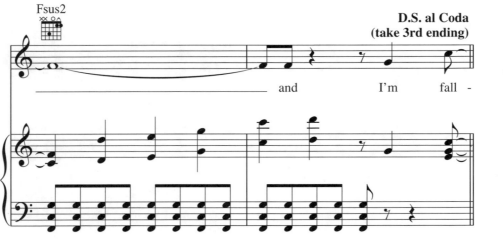

____ and I'm fall -

D.S. al Coda
(take 3rd ending)

CODA Csus2

(2.) *Vocals tacet*

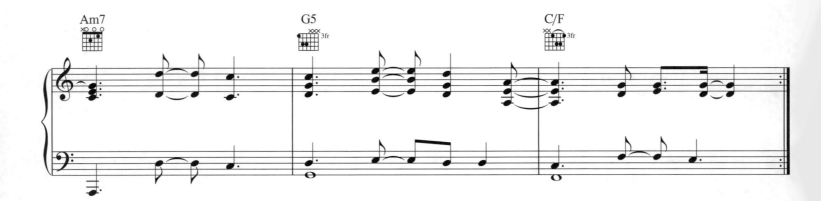

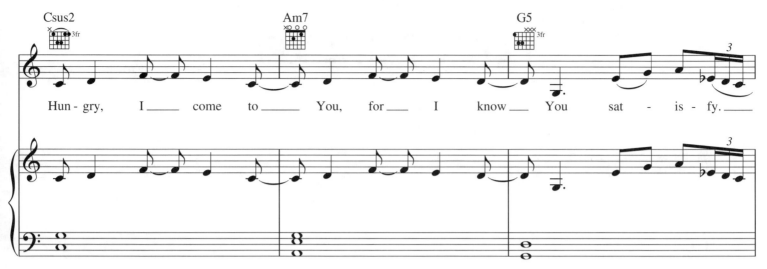

Hun - gry, I come to You, for I know You sat - is - fy.

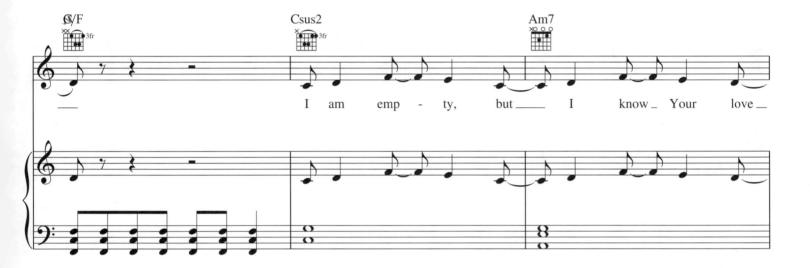

I am emp - ty, but I know Your love

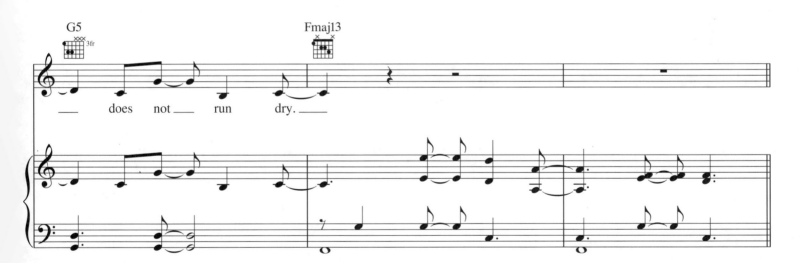

does not run dry.

Optional Ending

Repeat ad lib. and Fade

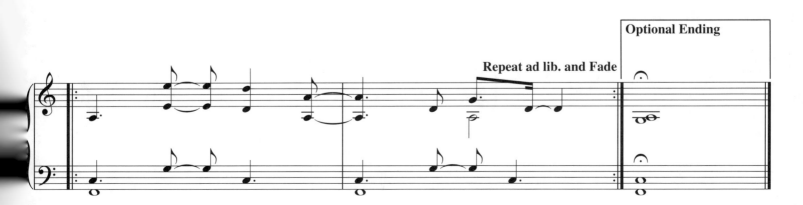

I COULD SING OF YOUR LOVE FOREVER

Words and Music by
MARTIN SMITH

Over the mountains and the sea Your river runs with love for me, and I will open up my heart and let the Healer set me free. I'm happy to be in the truth and I will daily lift my hands, for I will always sing of when Your love came down, yeah.

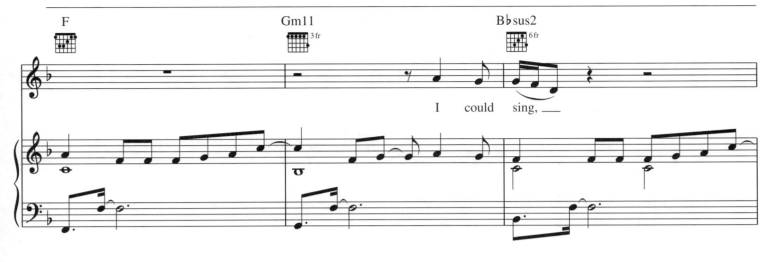

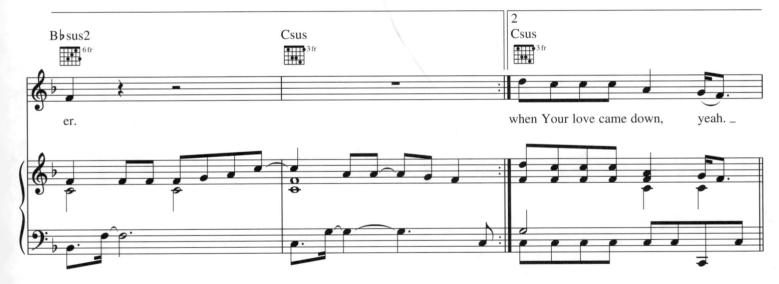

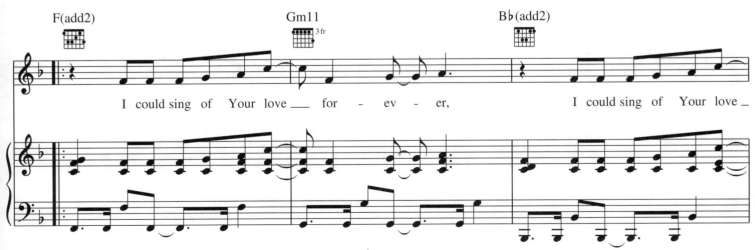

for - ev - er, ___ I could sing of Your love ___ for - ev - er,

I could sing of Your love ___ for - ev - er. ___ (I could sing of Your love ___

___ for - ev - er, I could sing of Your love ___ for - ev - er, ___

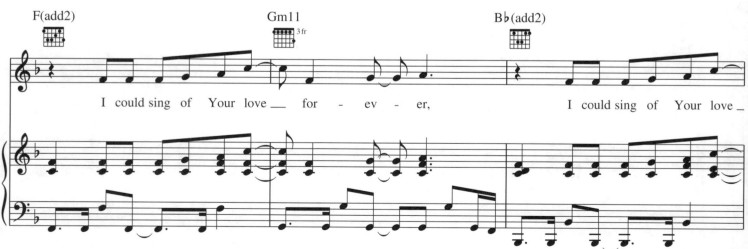

I could sing of Your love ___ for - ev - er, I could sing of Your love ___

I HAVE COME TO LOVE YOU

Words and Music by MARTIN COOPER
and PAUL OAKLEY

Moderately fast

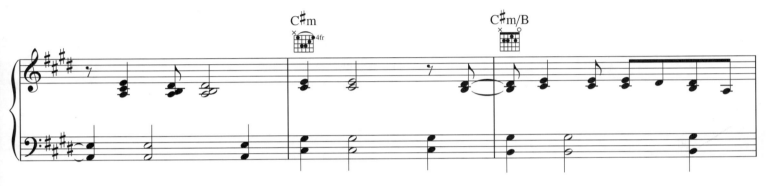

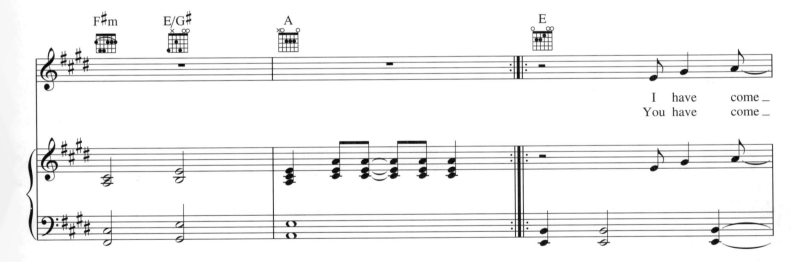

I have come __
You have come __

__ to love __ You,   for You have won __ my heart __
__ to love __ me   and heal my bro - ken heart. __

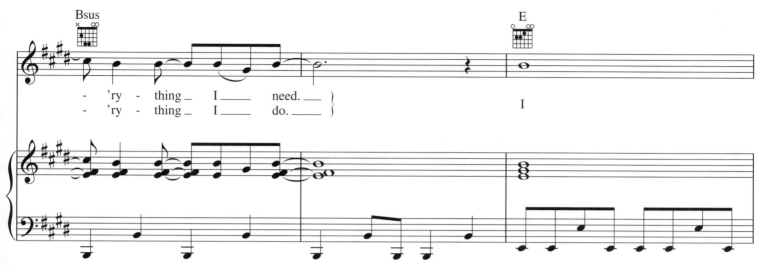

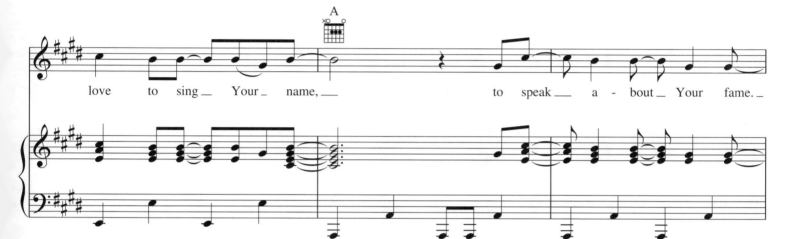

-'ry - thing __ I ____ need. ____
-'ry - thing __ I ____ do. ____

I

love to sing __ Your __ name, ____ to speak __ a - bout __ Your fame. __

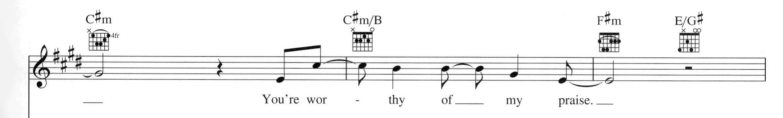

___ You're wor - thy of ___ my praise. __

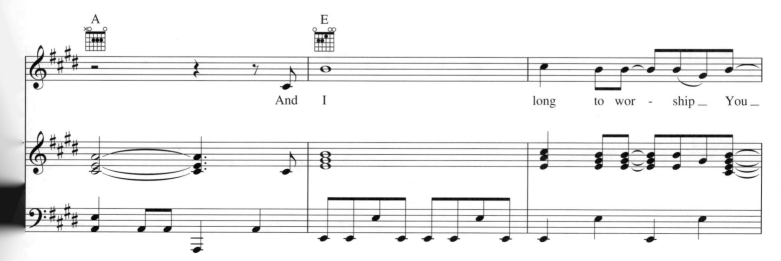

And I   long to wor - ship __ You __

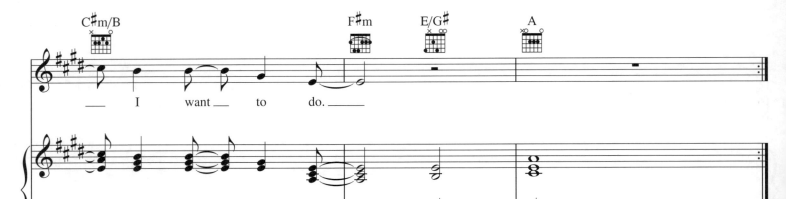

I will make _____ this gos - pel known. _____
Through me, let _____ Your king - dom come. _____

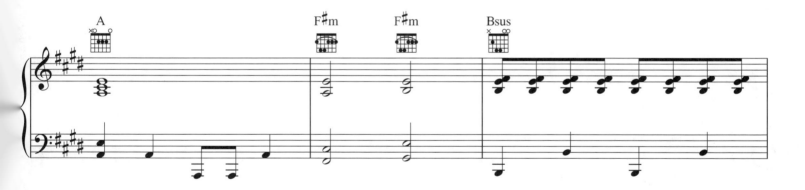

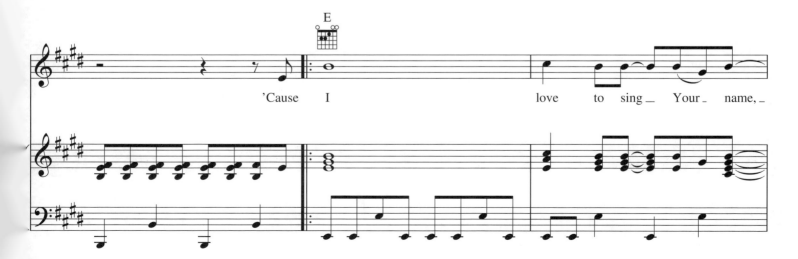

'Cause I love to sing _ Your _ name, _

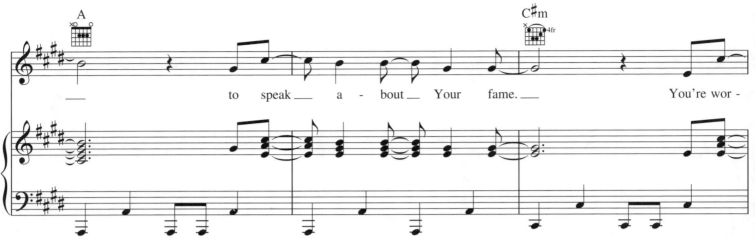

to speak __ a - bout __ Your fame. __ You're wor -

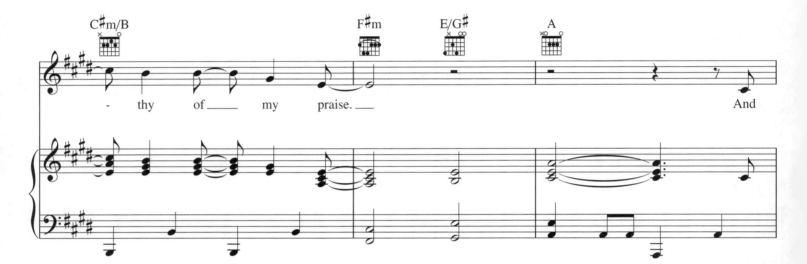

- thy of __ my praise. __ And

I long to wor - ship __ You __ in spir -

- it and __ in truth. __ It's all __

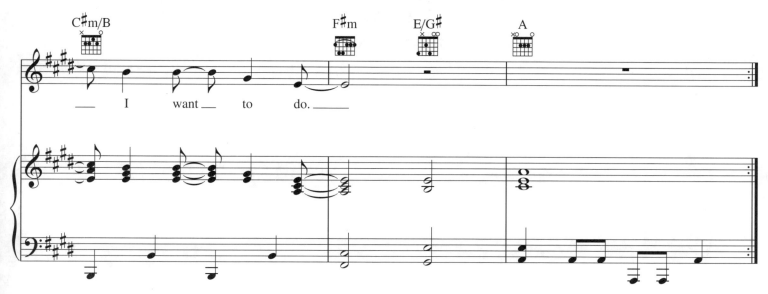

I want to do.

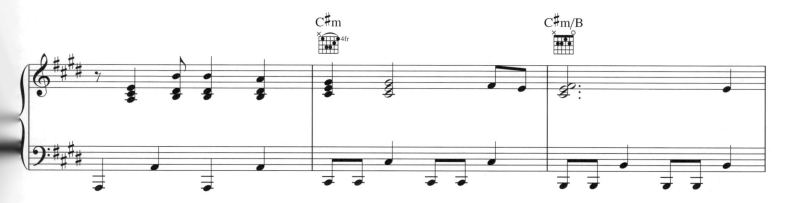

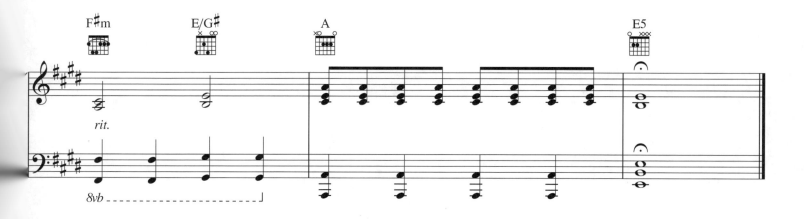

I WANT TO KNOW YOU
(In the Secret)

Words and Music by
ANDY PARK

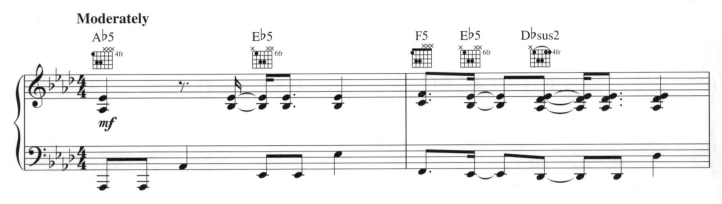

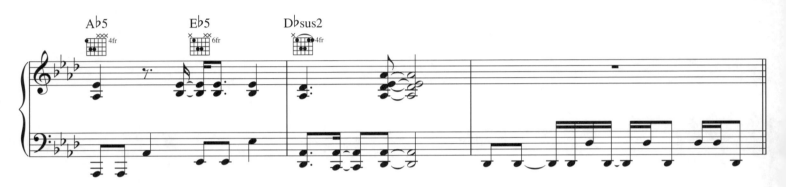

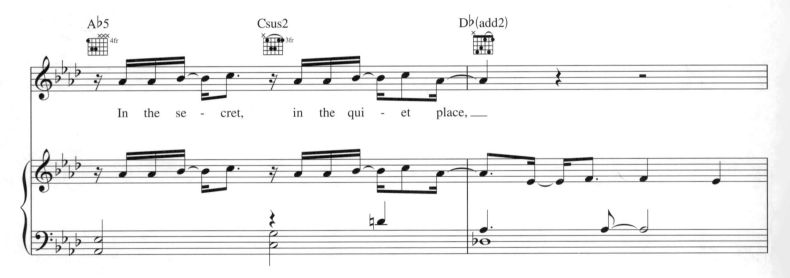

In the se - cret, in the qui - et place, ___

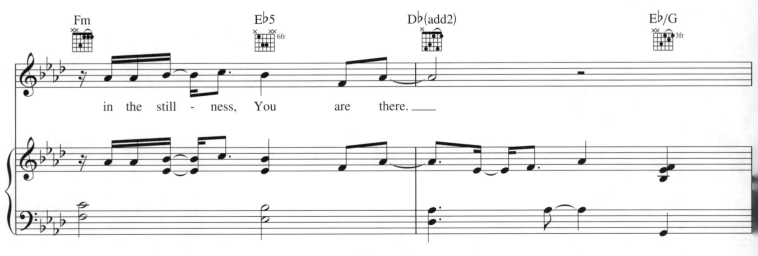

in the still - ness, You are there. ___

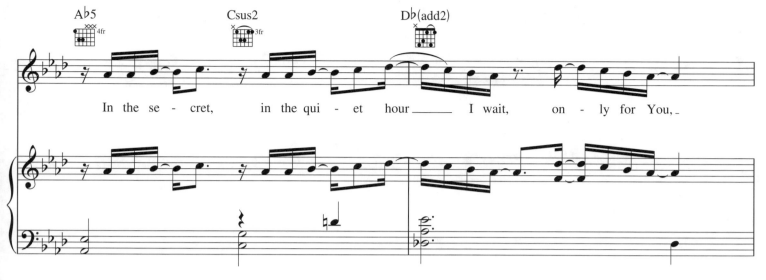

In the se - cret, in the qui - et hour ____ I wait, on - ly for You, _

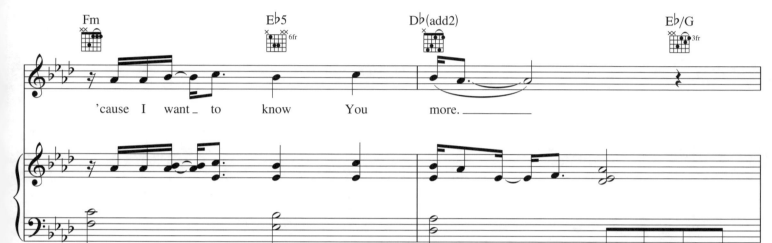

'cause I want _ to know You more. _____

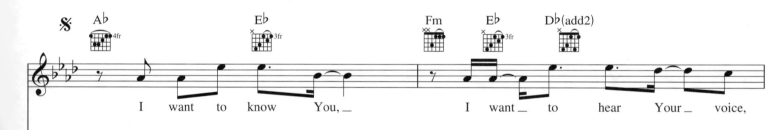

I want to know You, _ I want _ to hear Your _ voice,

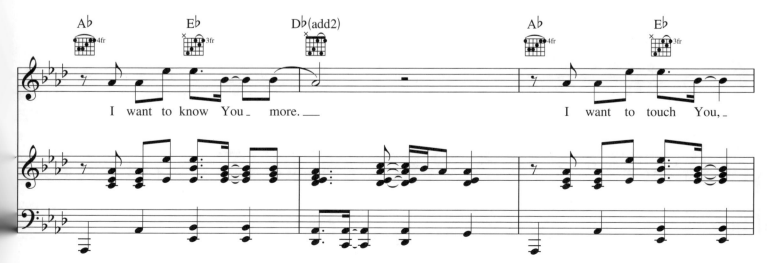

I want to know You _ more. ___ I want to touch You, _

I want to see Your face, I want to know You more.

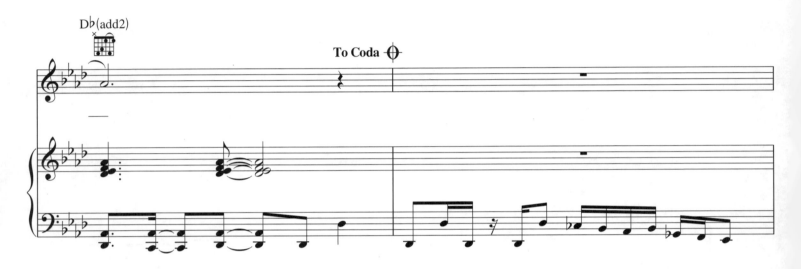

To Coda ⊕

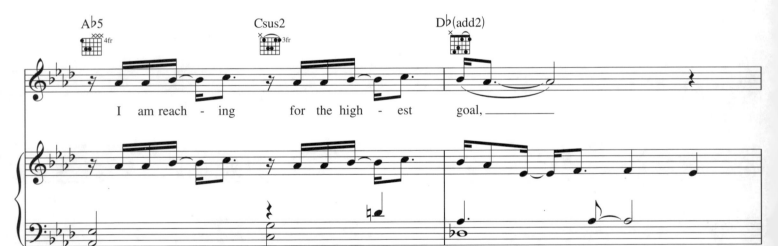

I am reach - ing for the high - est goal,

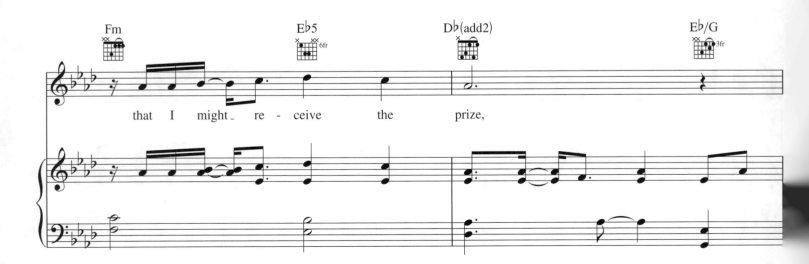

that I might re - ceive the prize,

I'VE FOUND JESUS

Words and Music by
MARTIN SMITH

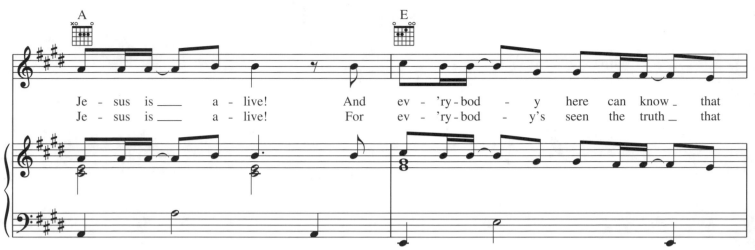

Je - sus is ___ a - live! And ev - 'ry - bod - y here can know ___ that
Je - sus is ___ a - live! For ev - 'ry - bod - y's seen the truth ___ that

Je - sus is ___ a - live! ___ }
Je - sus is ___ a - live! ___ } And I will live for all ___ my days

to raise the ban - ner of truth and light, ___ and

sing a - bout ___ my Sav - ior's love. And the best thing that hap - pened was the

JESUS, YOU ALONE

Words and Music by
TIM HUGHES

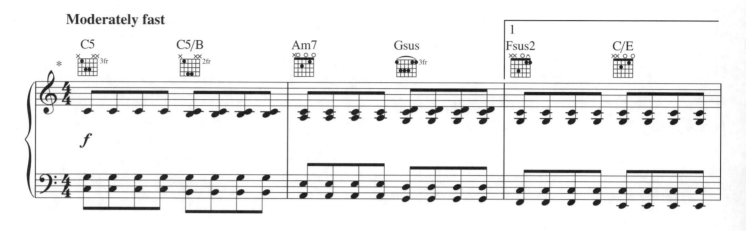

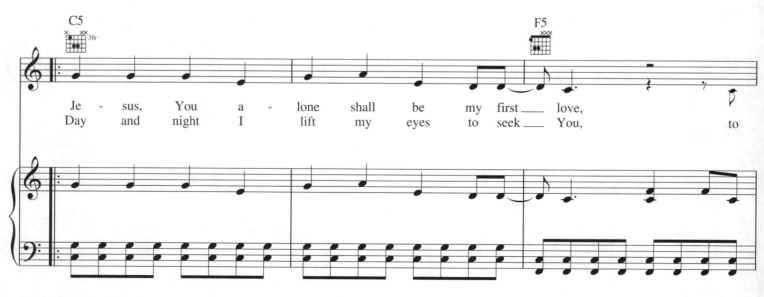

Je - sus, You a - lone shall be my first ___ love,
Day and night I lift my eyes to seek ___ You,

to

*Recorded a half step lower.

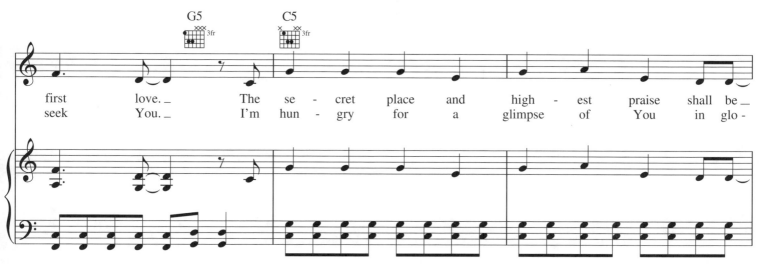

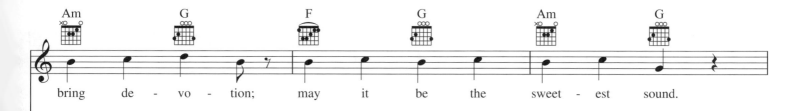

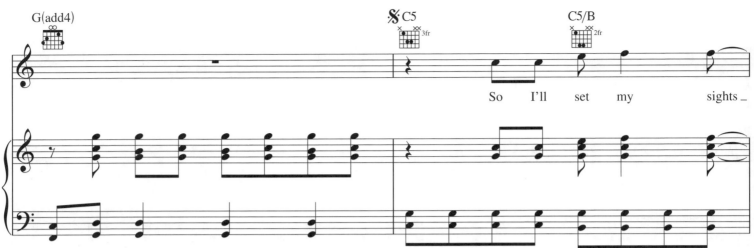

So I'll set my sights

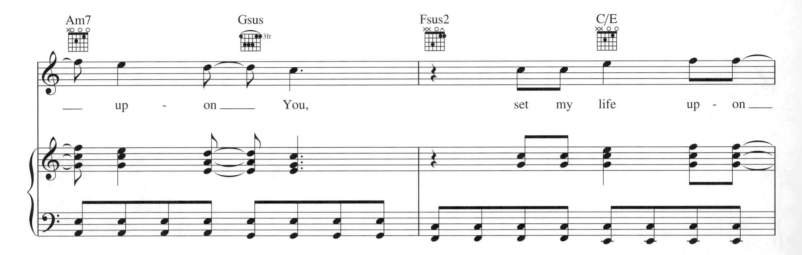

up - on You, set my life up - on

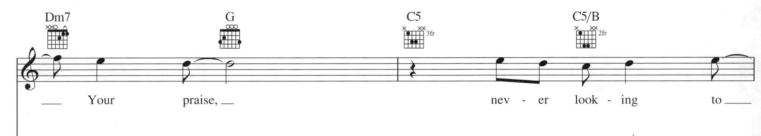

Your praise, never look - ing to

an - oth - er { (1.) way.
{ (2., D.S.) way,

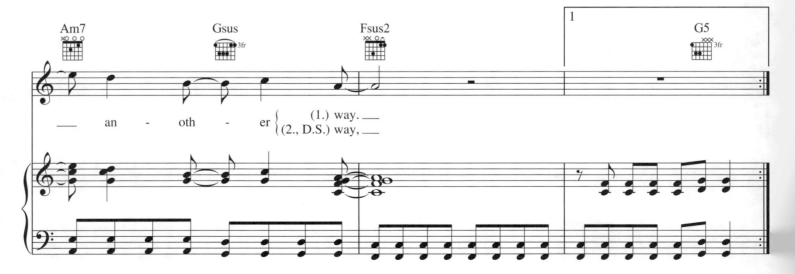

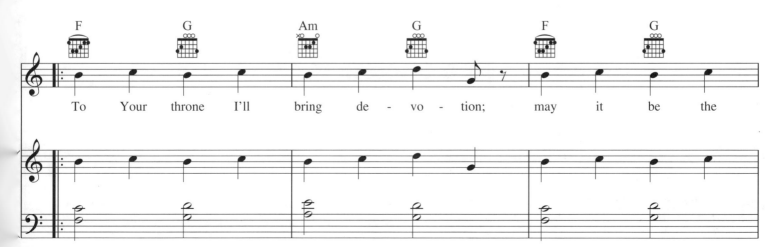

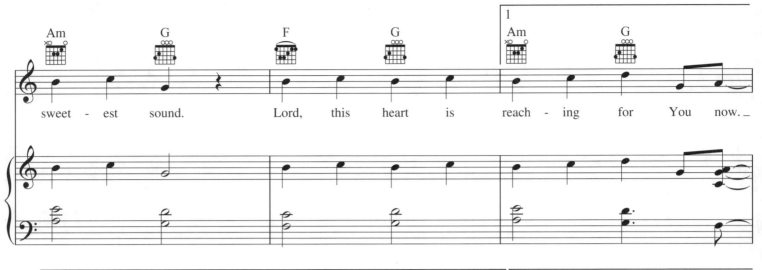

sweet - est sound. Lord, this heart is reach - ing for You now.

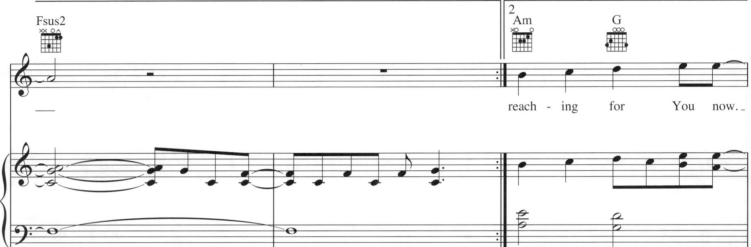

reach - ing for You now.

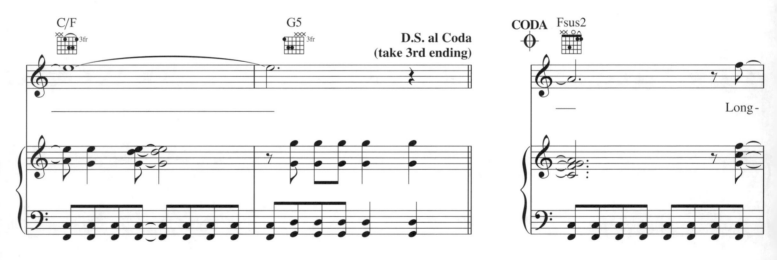

D.S. al Coda
(take 3rd ending)

CODA

Long -

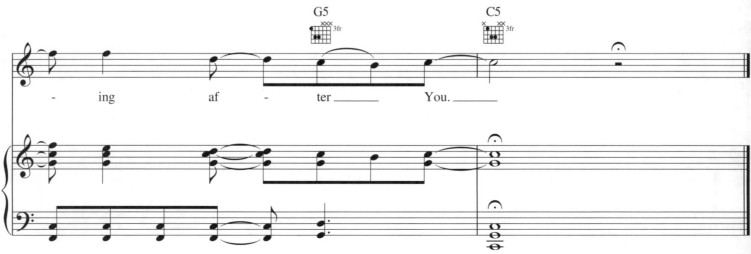

- ing af - ter You.

LET EVERYTHING THAT HAS BREATH

Words and Music by
MATT REDMAN

KINDNESS

Words and Music by LOUIE GIGLIO,
JESSE REEVES and CHRIS TOMLIN

Moderately slow

(1., 2.) O - pen up ____ the skies ____ of mer - cy
(3.) We can feel ____ Your mer - cy fall - ing.

and rain down ____ the cleans - ing ____ flood. ____
You are turn - ing our hearts back ____ a - gain.

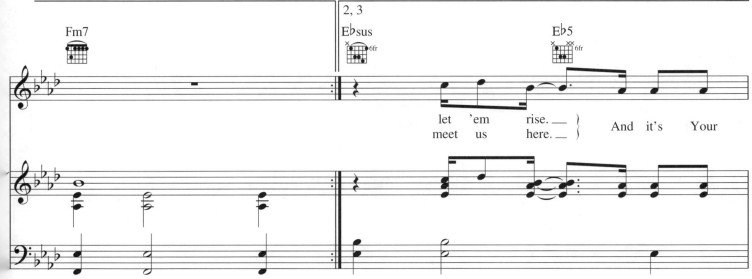

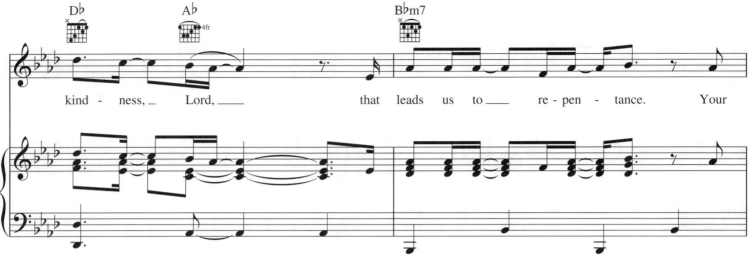

kind - ness,__ Lord,____ that leads us to__ re - pen - tance. Your

fa - vor,__ Lord,_____ is our de - sire._____ And it's Your

beau - ty,__ Lord,_____ that makes us stand__ in si - lence. Your__

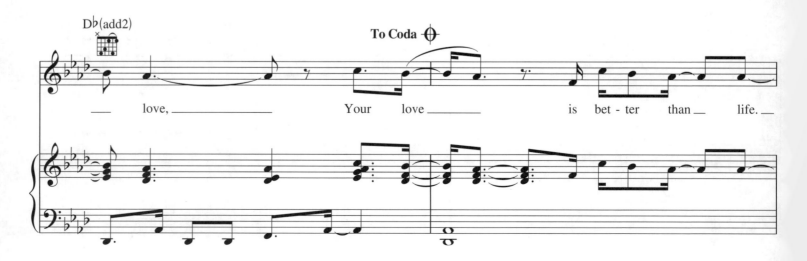

love,_____ Your love_____ is bet - ter than__ life.__

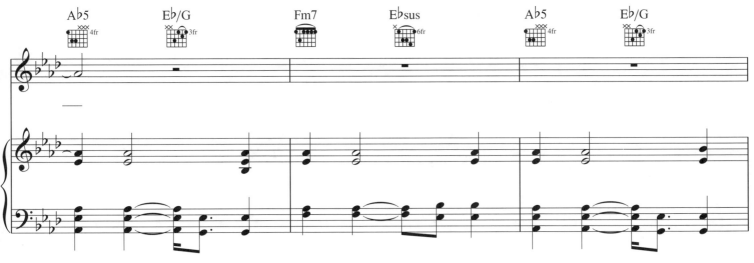

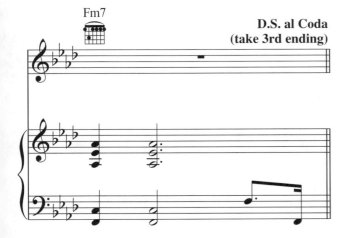

And it's Your

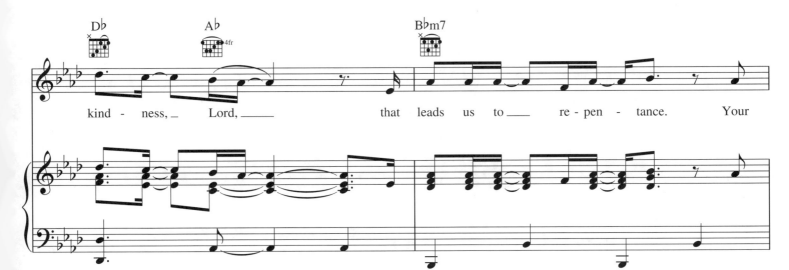

kind - ness, __ Lord, _____ that leads us to __ re - pen - tance. Your

fa - vor, __ Lord, _____ is our de - sire. _____ And it's Your

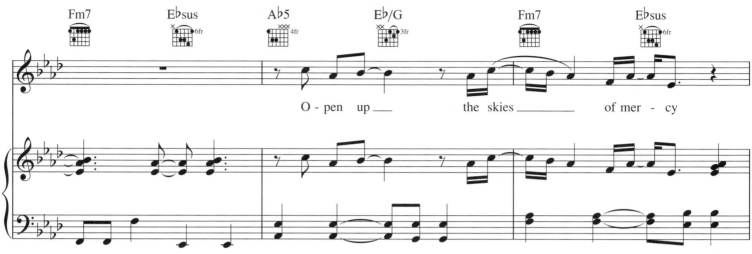

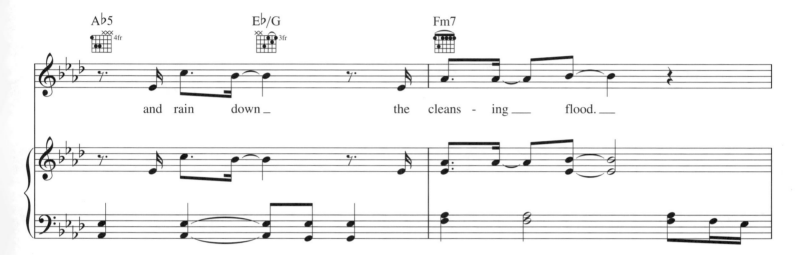

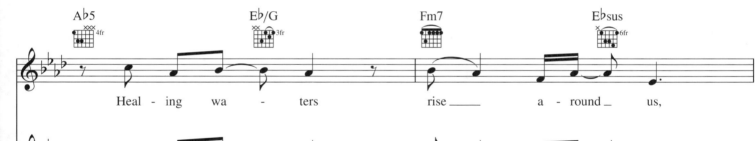

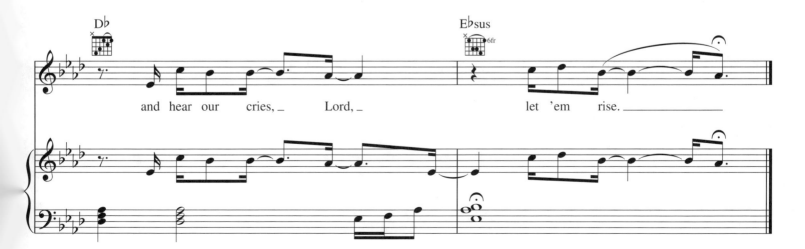

LET MY WORDS BE FEW
(I'll Stand in Awe of You)

Words and Music by MATT REDMAN
and BETH REDMAN

UNDIGNIFIED

Words and Music by
MATT REDMAN

Moderately fast

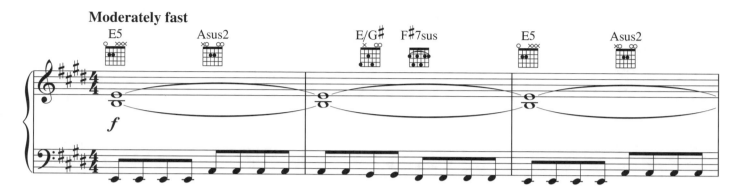

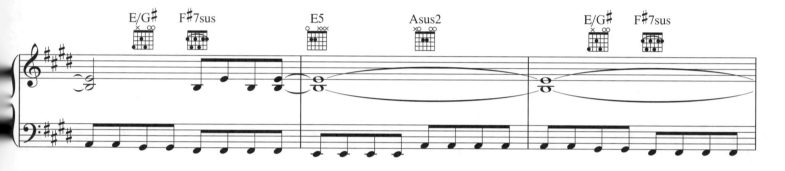

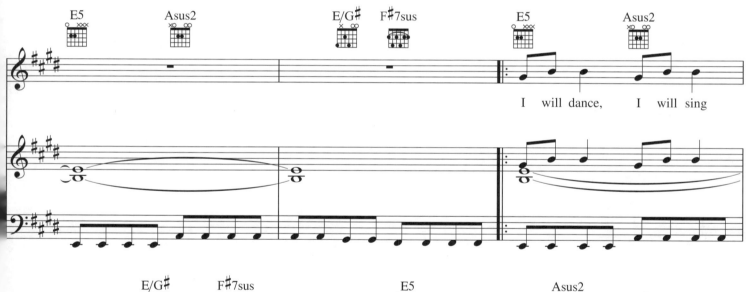

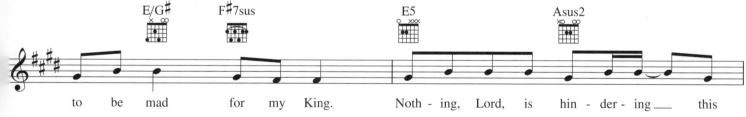

I will dance, I will sing

to be mad for my King. Noth-ing, Lord, is hin-der-ing this

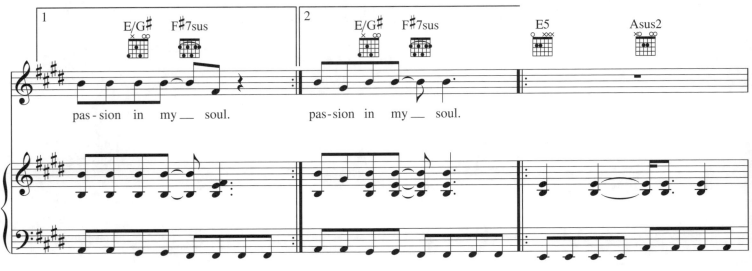

pas-sion in my __ soul.　　pas-sion in my __ soul.

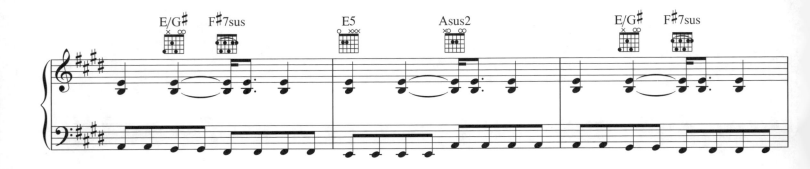

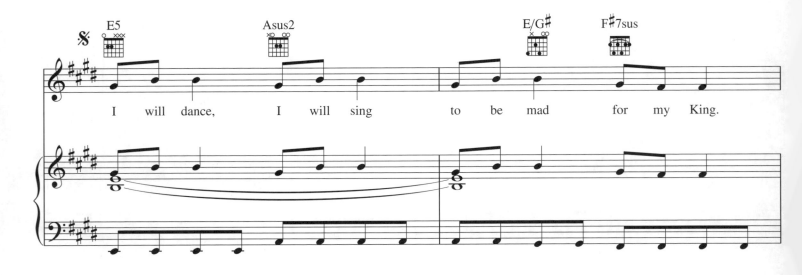

I will dance, I will sing to be mad for my King.

Noth-ing, Lord, is hin-der-ing __ this pas-sion in my __ soul.

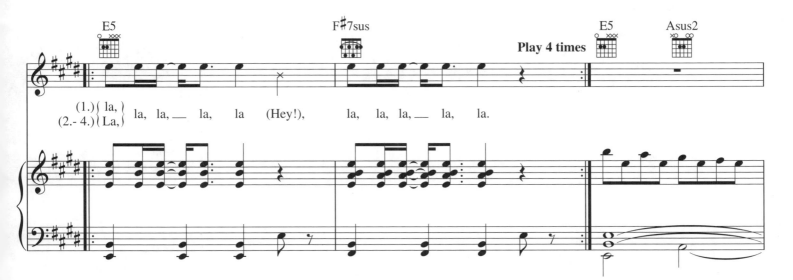

(1.) { la, } la, la,— la, la (Hey!), la, la, la,— la, la.
(2.-4.) { La, }

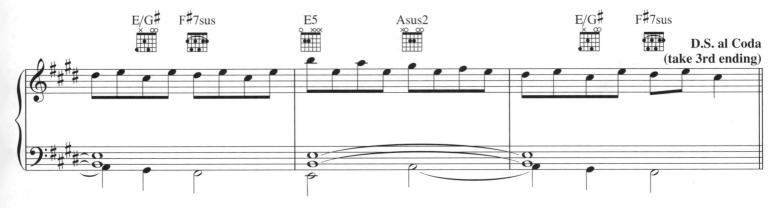

CODA

la, la, la. Sing la, la, la,— la, la (Hey!),

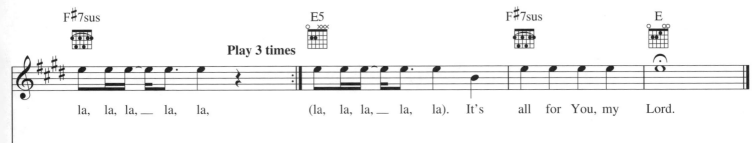

la, la, la,— la, la, (la, la, la,— la, la). It's all for You, my Lord.

LORD, YOU HAVE MY HEART

Words and Music by
MARTIN SMITH

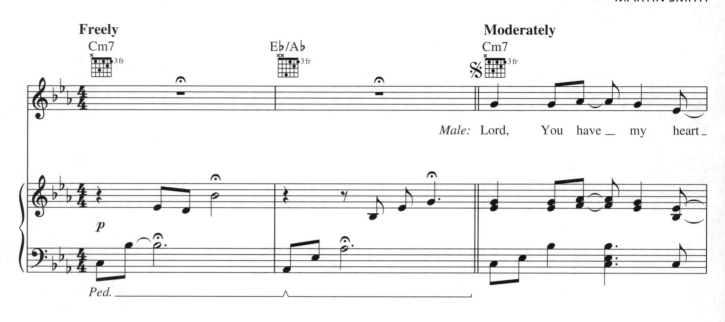

Male: Lord, You have __ my heart __

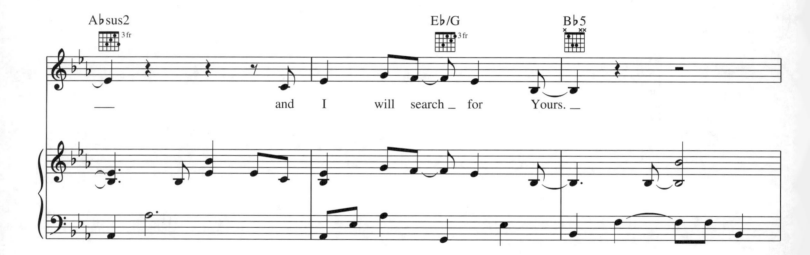

__ and I will search __ for Yours. __

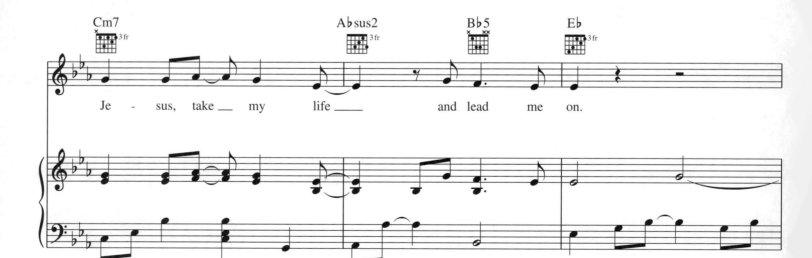

Je - sus, take __ my life ____ and lead me on.

Lord, You have ___ my heart ___ and

I will search ___ for Yours. ___ Let me be ___ to You ___

To Coda

___ a sac - ri - fice. And I will

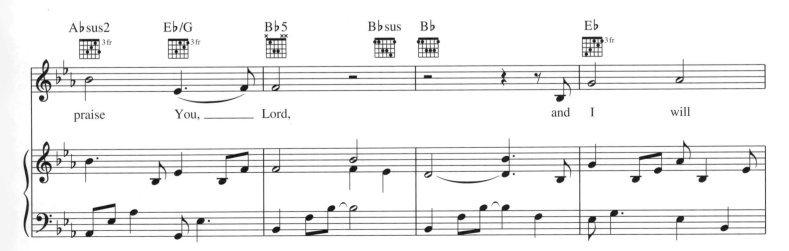

praise You, ___ Lord, and I will

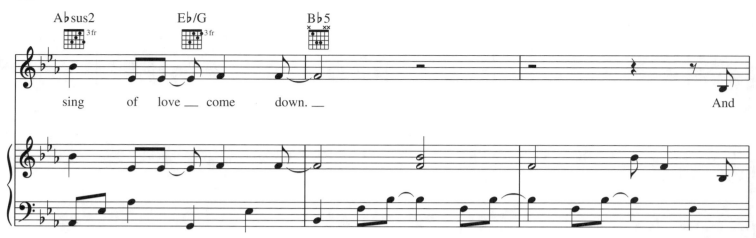

sing of love __ come down. __ And

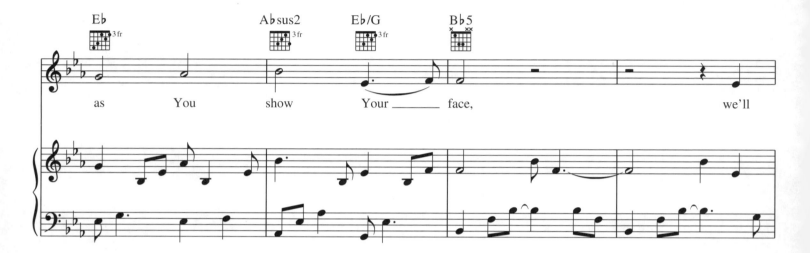

as You show Your _____ face, we'll

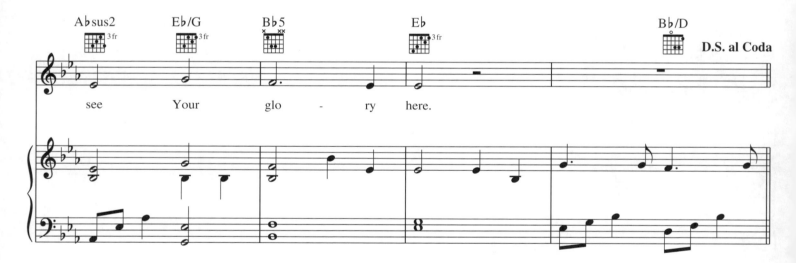

see Your glo - ry here.

D.S. al Coda

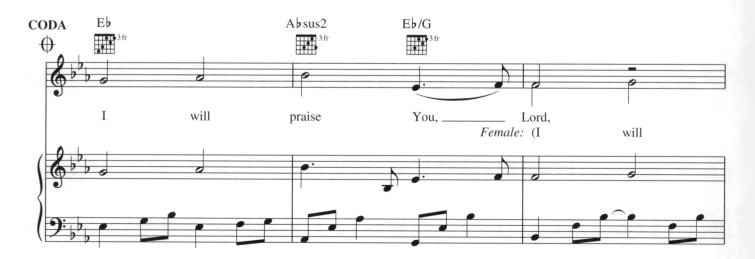

CODA

I will praise You, _____ Lord,

Female: (I will

MEET WITH ME

Words and Music by
LAMONT HIEBERT

Lyrics under the staves:

I'm here to meet with You.

Come and meet with me. I'm here to find

You. Re-veal Your-self to me. As I wait,

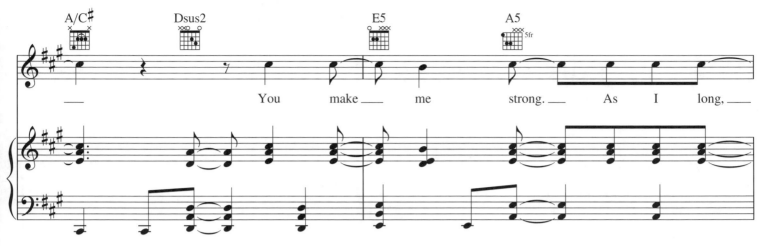

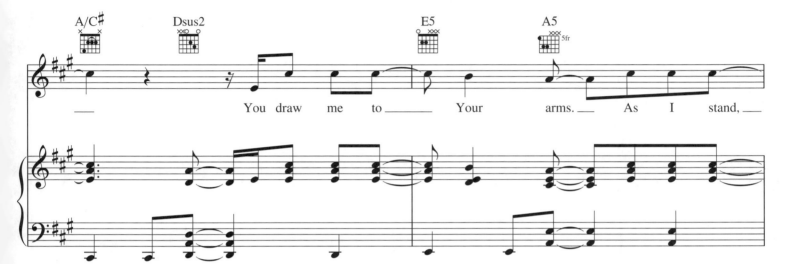

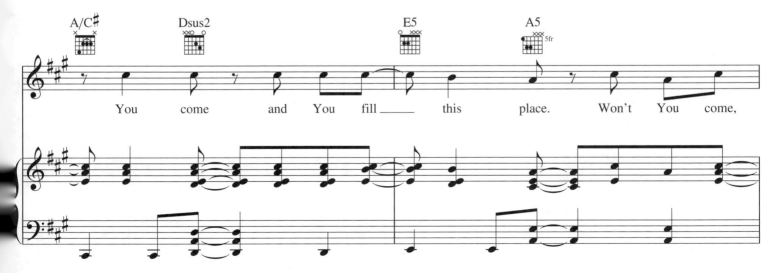

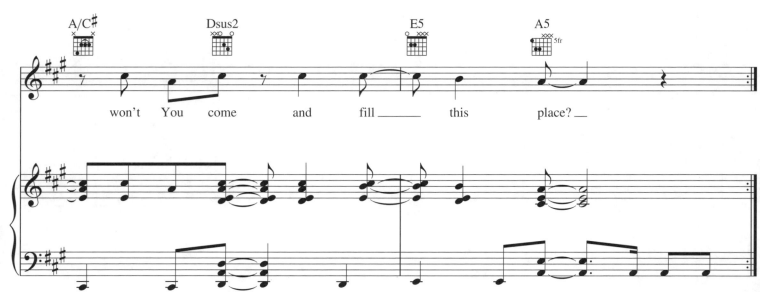

won't You come and fill _____ this place? __

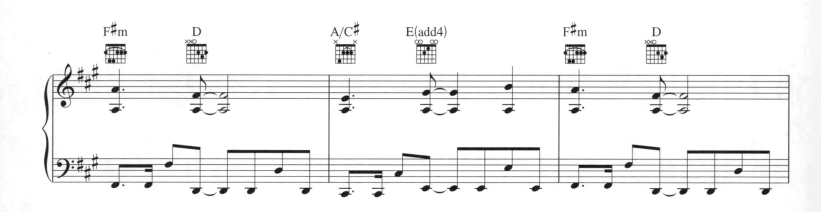

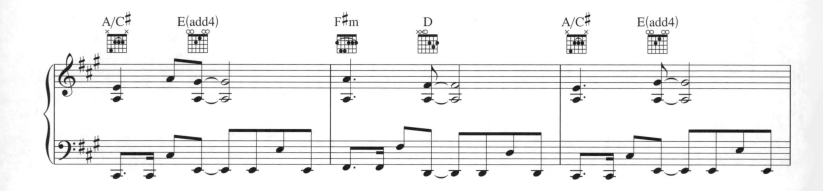

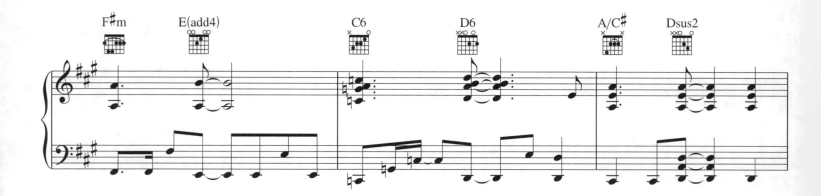

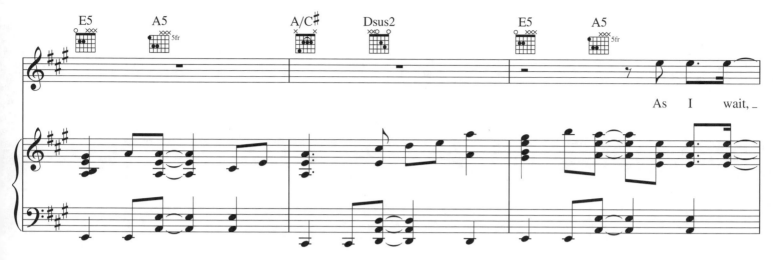

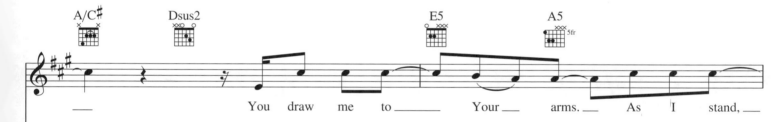

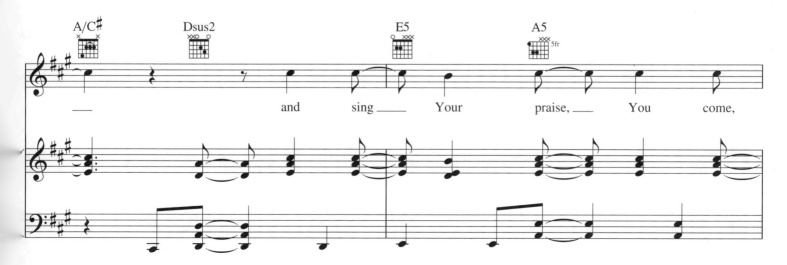

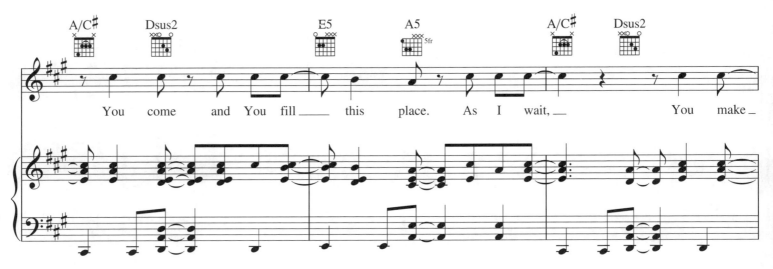

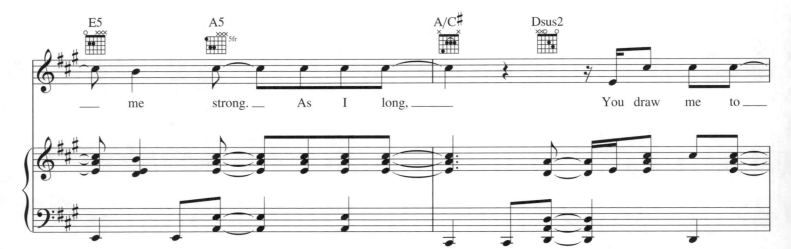

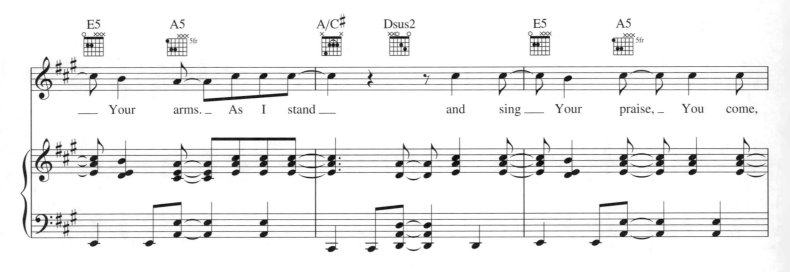

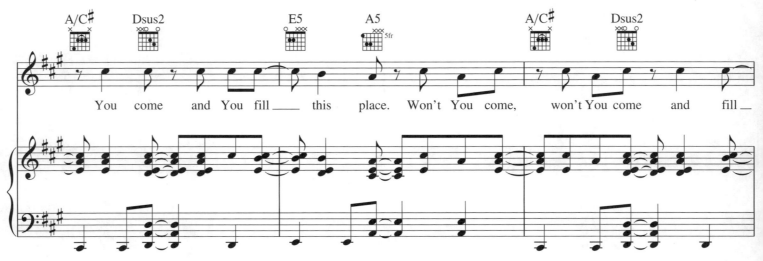

OPEN THE EYES OF MY HEART

Words and Music by
PAUL BALOCHE

Medium bright Pop

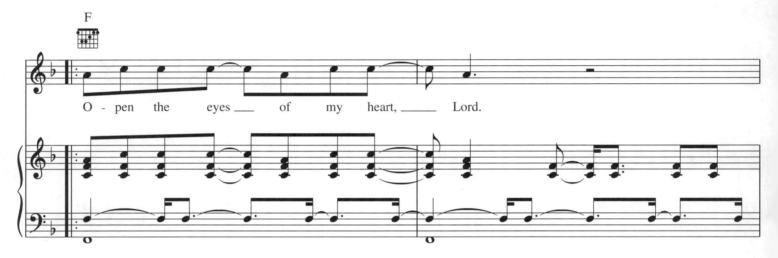

O - pen the eyes ___ of my heart, ___ Lord.

O - pen the eyes ___ of my heart. ___ I want _ to

see ___ You. _ I want _ to see ___ You. _

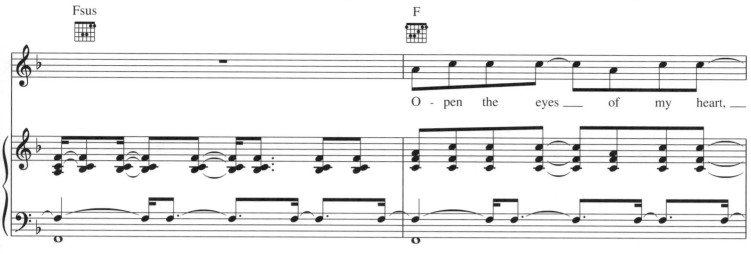

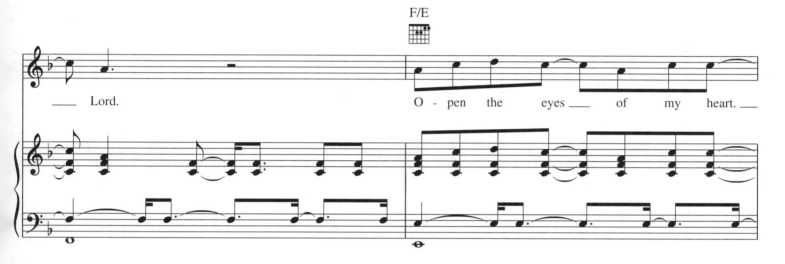

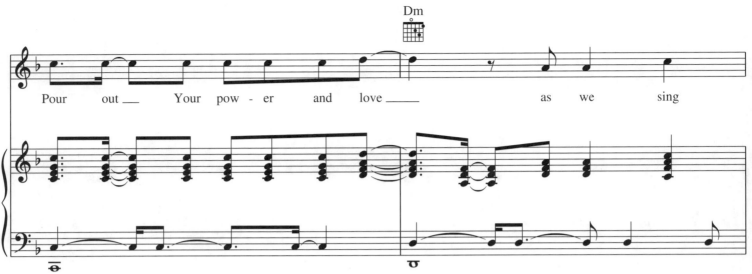

Pour out __ Your pow-er and love __ as we sing

ho-ly ho - ly, ho - ly. __

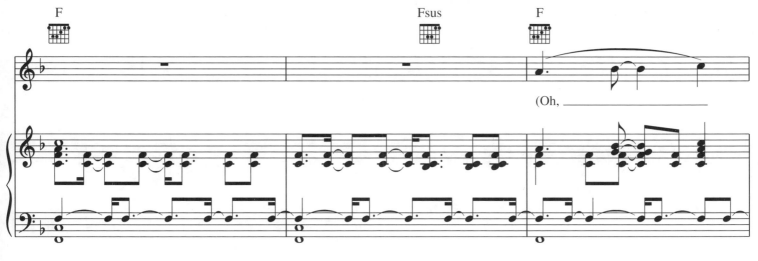

(Oh, _____

ho - ly, ___ oh, _____ ho - ly, ___

oh, _____ ho - ly, I want to see You.) _

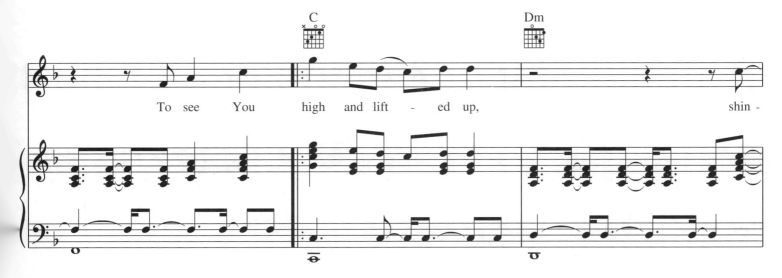

To see You high and lift - ed up, shin -

SALVATION

Words and Music by
CHARLIE HALL

With excitement

Sal - va - tion, spring up from __ the ground, Lord, rend the heav - ens and __ come down, seek the lost __ and heal __ the lame; Je - sus bring glo - ry to __ Your name. Let all the

prod - i - gals __ run home, all of cre - a - tion waits __ and groans. Lord, we've heard __

__ of Your __ great fame; Fa - ther, cause all to shout __ Your name.

Stir up our hearts, ___ oh ___ God; ___

o - pen our spir - its to awe ___ who You are. __

__ Put a cry ___ in ___ us so ___ deep _

__ in - side that we can - not find the ___ words _

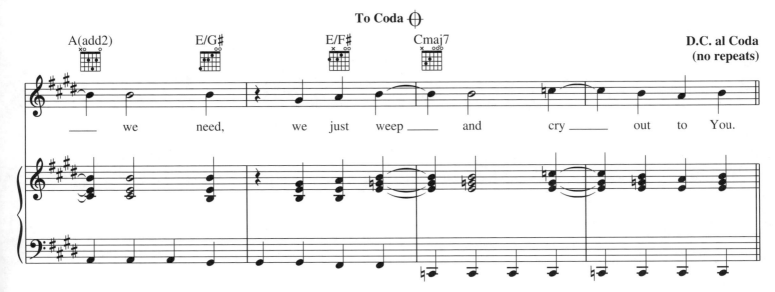

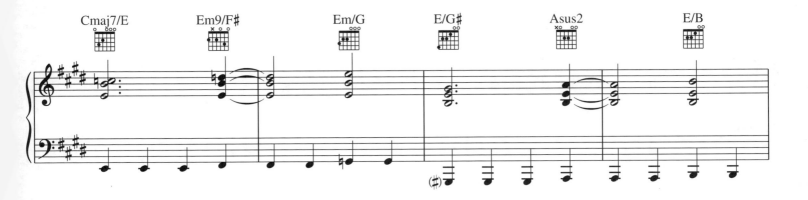

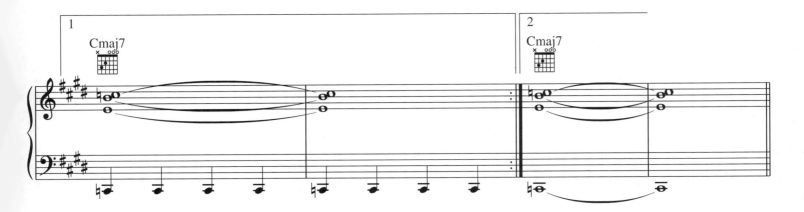

Lord, we've heard ___ of Your ___ great fame; Fa - ther, cause

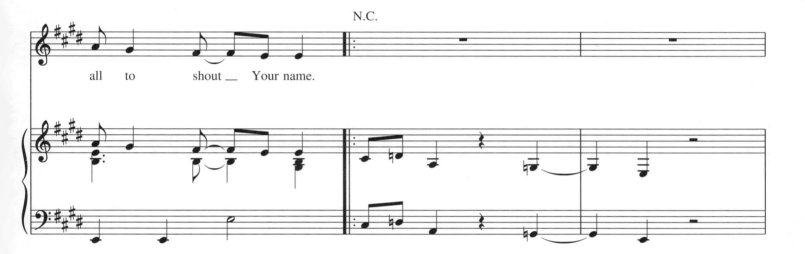

all to shout ___ Your name.

Repeat and Fade   **Optional Ending**

YOU ALONE

Words and Music by JACK PARKER
and DAVID CROWDER

(1., 3.) You _____ are the on - ly _____ one I _____ need. _____ I bow
(2., 4.) You _____ have giv - en me _____ more than _____ I _____ could

all of me _____ at Your _____ feet. _____ I
ev - er have _____ want - ed, _____ and I _____ want to

wor - ship _____ You a - lone.
give You my _____ heart and my _____ soul.

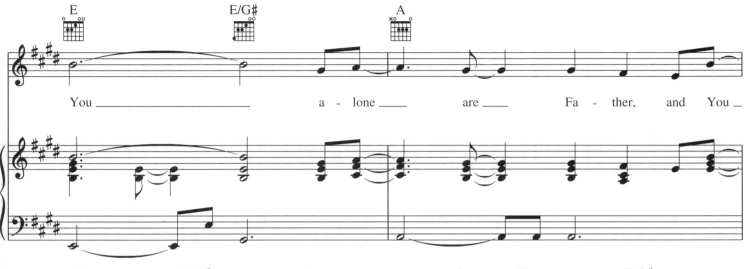

You _____ a - lone _____ are _____ Fa - ther, and You _

_____ a - lone ___ are ___ good. You _____ a - lone _

To Coda

_____ are _____ Sav - ior, and You _____ a - lone _

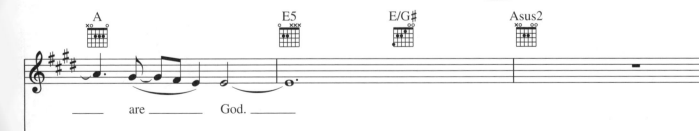

_____ are _____ God. _____

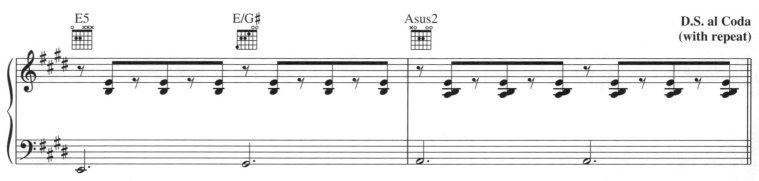

D.S. al Coda
(with repeat)

YOU ARE MY KING
(Amazing Love)

Words and Music by
BILLY JAMES FOOTE

Worshipfully

I'm for-giv-en _____ be-cause You were _ for-sak-en.

I'm ac-cept-ed; You were _ con-demned. _ I'm a-live _ and well; _ Your

Spir-it is ___ with-in ___ me be-cause You died _ and rose _ a-gain. _